MORE
MONOLOGUES
ON
BLACK LIFE

MORE MONOLOGUES ON BLACK LIFE

Gus Edwards

HEINEMANN
Portsmouth, NH

Heinemann
A division of Reed Elsevier Inc.
361 Hanover Street
Portsmouth, NH 03801–3912
www.heinemanndrama.com

Offices and agents throughout the world

Performance rights information can be found on p. 159.

Library of Congress Cataloging-in-Publication Data
Edwards, Gus.
    More monologues on Black life / Gus Edwards.
        p. cm.
    ISBN 0–325–00289–4 (alk. paper)
        1. Afro-Americans—Drama. 2. City and town life—United
States—Drama. 3. Monologues. I. Title.

    PS3555.D925 M67 2000
    812'.54—dc21   00-029565

Editor: Lisa A. Barnett
Production: Vicki Kasabian
Cover design: Joni Doherty
Author photo: Jon Simpson Photography
Manufacturing: Deanna Richardson

Printed in the United States of America on acid-free paper
04 03 02 01 00   VP   1 2 3 4 5

Contents

Foreword

Within the pages of this modestly titled book, you will find a treasure trove of short yet complete one-person plays by one of America's finest Black playwrights. This unique compilation of fifty short one-person plays provides a wealth of material for actors in search of well-written monologues from the Black experience. The variety of African American male and female characters, ranging in age from the late teens to the sixties, is extraordinary. It will be the rare actor who is not able to find a stirring monologue that is age and gender appropriate within these covers.

In *More Monologues on Black Life,* as in his many earlier works, Gus Edwards has created characters who are remarkably true to themselves—whether they are blatantly flawed, or quietly heroic. Whatever their condition in life, they speak openly and unabashedly in the censure-free atmosphere that Edwards establishes. It was this arresting quality of his writing that first caught the attention of Douglas Turner Ward, artistic director and cofounder of the prestigious Negro Ensemble Company. Ward was sufficiently impressed by Gus Edwards' writing to produce not only his first play, *The Offering,* but also another of his plays, *Black Body Blues,* in the same 1977–78 NEC season. Subsequently, he also named Gus Edwards resident playwright at the NEC. Almost twenty years later, Ward still reminisces about *The Offering* in his introduction to *Classic Plays from the Negro Ensemble Company* (coedited by Gus Edwards and Paul Carter Harrison). Ward recalls that "[t]he chilling narratives, casual verbal violence, self-contained nonconventional [sic] conduct, and engulfing sexuality were so riveting . . ." (6).

Since his NEC beginnings, Gus Edwards has created an enviable body of work ranging from full-length stage plays such as *Weep Not for Me* and *Ramona* to the acclaimed screen adaptation of James Baldwin's *Go Tell It on the Mountain.* Simultaneously, he has also embraced and mastered the art of the monologue. Both his play, *Lifetimes on the Streets,* and his first volume of monologues entitled *Monologues on Black Life* attest to Edwards' intense artistic interest in this form. Indeed, the monologue has become the cornerstone to Edwards' artistic ambitions. In the introduction to *Monologues on Black Life,* he even states, "In my more ambitious moments I like to think that I'm in the process of creating an enormous theatrical mosaic of black American life through monologues" (xi).

With *More Monologues on Black Life,* Edwards adventures still closer to the realization of this ambition. Organized into six sections—We Is Who We Want to Be; Moody's Mood Café; The Projects; The Sorrows of Elva; Rap Talk; and Five Black Heroes in Monologues—this collection of monologues depicts a plethora of African American characters, lifestyles, and stories loosely gathered around themes, states of mind, or physical settings. The most eclectic section is the first, We Is Who We Want to Be. Typical of Edwards' characters, the sixteen people portrayed in this section are struggling with the bewildering twists and turns of the human condition. The meek become violent; the abused become targetless haters; soldiers become evangelists and panhandlers; hypocrites find success in their deceit, and fantasy lovers triumph over real men. Yet in the midst of all of this human chaos can be heard strains of hope, love, and affirmation of human dignity. Above all, in contrast to the limited depictions found in the media, this section is a celebration of the myriad of Black life experiences.

In juxtaposition to the more free-ranging nature of the first section, the eight monologues in Moody's Mood Café are connected by a shared state of mind. A bartender, Nunez, frames the section with his third-person narrative about a recently deceased African American Catholic Monsignor who used to appear regularly first thing in the morning and the last thing at night for his Johnny Walker Black. The rest of the monologues are in the blues voice of those whose pained experiences have compelled them to seek the solace of liquor. The stories vary widely from a woman who poisoned her husband because he was sexually abusing their daughter to a young man who has let his fantasies of the "good life" overwhelm his sense of reality.

The third section is simply entitled The Projects. While the monologues in Moody Mood's Café are connected to a location primarily by their "mood," the monologues in this section are anchored by the inner city experience of project living. Gus Edwards says in his prologue to this section, "The Projects of the big cities is where so many of us live out our lives. . . . We live here, we die here, and in between we reach for a memory, reach for a dream. Or sometimes we just stand still and wait . . . for the future to happen." These ten monologues mainly articulate complex, troubled, and troubling love relationships but there is also some colorful nostalgia about the projects "back in the day" and about 42d Street before the Disney invasion.

In the fourth section, Edwards explores a slightly different form. The Sorrows of Elva is one monologue in six parts. While each part, or "sorrow," can stand alone and function beautifully as a discrete monologue, there is a plotline that links the six sorrows. Together they tell the poignant story of the experiences of the twenty-seven-year-old Elva. Having married a good man who is loving, supportive, but not romantically exciting, Elva strays into an extramarital relationship and pregnancy only to be salvaged in the end by her husband's abiding love and his undaunted sense of "Don't worry, everthing gon work out."

In a very different twist, section five is precisely what it says—Rap Talk. These five monologues for actors in their late teens or early twenties are poems rapping about literal and figurative paralysis. Several of the characters expound about and illustrate the dangers of actual physical paralysis as a result of drunk driving or party horseplay. Another rapper tries to entice his listeners with drugs, another potential source of paralysis of the will and self-control. Taking the theme even further, the last rapper looks historically at the paralysis of free will for African Americans as an inherent tragic part of the American tradition of slavery.

The last section, Five Black Heroes, is devoted to portrayals of five important figures from the annals of African American history. With these monologues about Frederick Douglass, Mahalia Jackson, Buddy Bolden, Coretta Scott, and James Baldwin, Edwards provides the opportunity for actors to portray characters whose stature is heightened and deepened by the resonance of their actual historical presence. To further ground the monologues in the context of their personal lives, Edwards also provides brief biographies. As might be expected, the monologues vary in tone. The great orator Frederick Douglass speaks movingly on slavery, the vote, and women's suffrage. A major voice of the Black Civil Rights Movement, James Baldwin orates about waiting for "the dream of America's deliverance to become a reality." Mahalia Jackson and Buddy Bolden, two giants in the music world, relate moments in their lives in more personal tones, as if responding to an interview or, perhaps in the case of Buddy Bolden, to a friend or acquaintance. Also in this quieter vein is Coretta Scott King's monologue, which stands out poignantly for its touching reminiscence of one small personal moment with Martin Luther King Jr. prior to his acceptance of the Nobel Peace for Peace.

The personal narratives, organized in these sections,

make *More Monologues on Black Life* not only a compelling collection of monologues but also an impressive volume of first-person short stories. However, literary considerations aside, first and foremost these are theatrical pieces, designed to be spoken and performed. As such, the organization makes it quickly obvious that the monologues in each division could make a good theatrical evening. Yet Edwards' choice of organization is not meant to hinder reconceptualizations and regroupings. Edwards even notes in his introduction to *Monologues on Black Life:* "Over the years I've seen them performed in a variety of ways and in a variety of places. Theatres, schools, coffee shops, bookstores, museums and even in nightclubs. The combinations are always surprising. Sometimes they're linked thematically or by gender or however else the presenter deems fit. The lengths, too, have varied from fifteen to ninety minutes and all the stops in between. It then occurred to me that I had stumbled upon a very flexible form, so I continued and will continue writing this way. . . . Monologues are my life" (x, xi). Because of Gus Edwards' love of the monologue, actors, readers, and producers have, in this volume, still another gallery of marvelous Black portraits to add to their repertory of dramatic literature.

Beth Turner

WE IS WHO WE WANT TO BE

Throughout our history as a people in this land someone is always trying to tell us who to be, what to say, how to think, how to walk, how to dress and even how to speak. "Don't say *dis,*' say *this.*" Don't say *dem,*' say *those.*" What they don't seem to understand is that *We Is Who We Want to Be.* And in that choice is where freedom lives.

Just Cause

Lorraine, thirties

I get so mad at myself thinking what a fool I was. Listening to that man telling me how sexually limited I was. And worse than listening, I believed that man. Can you imagine that! I believed the SOB. After all, why would he lie? We were married and deeply in love, weren't we? So I went along with this scheme of his to introduce a third party to our lives and our bed. Her name was Jody. And she seemed likable enough. He brought her home to dinner so that we could all get acquainted. She didn't look like much to me and didn't say much either. But I wasn't a man, so what did I know? And all he kept whispering to me was "You can learn a lot from her. She's a very free person." I looked at this urchin and couldn't figure out what my husband was talking about. What could I learn from a girl who looked and talked like she hadn't even gotten out of high school? Still, I didn't say anything. Why?

Because I really wanted to go through with it. Believe me when I tell you that. That's how stupid and trusting I was. I wasn't doing something right in my marriage and I wanted to correct it. So we began preparing for the event. But the closer we got the more doubts I had. Finally, I said to Ernie, "Darling, I'm sorry but I just can't go through with it. I don't know what it is. Maybe it's my inhibition or my upbringing, but I just can't and I'm sorry."

Well, he turned to me and said, "Lorraine, you know what your problem is? You're a tightass. That's what you are, an uptight, constipated tightass." Then he turned to the girl Jody and said, "Baby, I'm sorry." Can you picture that? He apologized to this black bimbo because I wouldn't let her join us in bed. (*Pause*)

Well, I guess something inside me must've just exploded because I started screaming and throwing things. The girl Jody wasn't as dumb as she looked. Because soon as the shouting began she ran out the front door. But Ernie just stood there with his hand out saying "What's the matter with you? Huh? What's wrong with you? Cool it. Cool it," while I was smashing furniture and glassware all around him.

Now I didn't mean to hit him with the lamp and crack his skull open like I did. No, I didn't mean to do that at all. It happened in the heat of things. I threw the lamp, his head was there and Slam! Bam! Ali Kazam! He was on the floor calling out, "Oh my God, oh my God. You killed me. You killed me." . . . Of course he wasn't dead. That man was always overdramatizing. But still, I'm here in jail and you're here trying to defend me.

I don't say I'm innocent, but I don't think I'm guilty either. I had just cause. And if you as my lawyer can't make the judge understand that, then I got another lamp waiting for your head, too. And that ain't a threat. That, Mister, is a promise.

The Imposter

Dennis, late thirties

When people start to talk religion, I automatically turn off. The minute I hear them going on about God this, God that, I have one of two thoughts. Either the person speaking is a fool, or they think I am. The pattern of existence is too problematical, too mysterious, too full of contradictions and complexities to be simply explained by the mindless pieties of most organized religions, Christian or otherwise. If questioned further, I'd even go so far as to say that religion from my view of things is probably the most dangerous and effective political tool ever devised by man. It purports to have the big answers, which in our heart of hearts we know nobody knows, and insists not only that we follow behind and serve it but that we do so on blind faith. Not via reason, logic, or persuasion. But faith. Pure, mindless faith. And when one refuses to do so, then of course you're weak, contrary, and perhaps potentially dangerous.

Even the language of religion indicates its attitude towards the faithful. We're constantly hearing talk about shepherds, sheep, or flock. If the minister, priest, preacher, or whoever insists on referring to himself (sometimes herself) as "our shepherd" then of course the only thing expected from us is that we follow in obedient docile fashion, occasionally saying, "Baa . . . baa . . . baa . . . baa." And if you think I'm wrong, the next time you go to church, try asking questions about the scriptures, about the motives behind the minister's words or about the reason that church exists. What you'll raise are hackles. What you will ultimately have to deal with is hostility and the observation or warning that you've got to watch yourself, your faith is becoming shaky.

Religion since time began has been the vehicle which has allowed one man to lead a multitude into whatever direction he chooses. Sometime it's been for good. Oftentimes not. Religion became the drug that kept the American slaves in line. They were told that although their condition on Earth—actually here in the good old US of A—was dismal, there was a greater place they were headed where all rights would be wronged and the virtues of non-rebellion and obedience would be greatly rewarded. In fact, they even went so far as to explain that the greater your suffering here, the greater, proportionally speaking, your reward "up there" would be. And it worked. It worked so wonderfully well that for nearly two hundred years you had no serious questioning or response against the status quo. And the few who did try to rebel, besides being mutilated, slaughtered, or hung were also condemned as that most heinous of all things, "godless."

My surprise was that we didn't learn to use that weapon religion against our oppressors, in and out of slavery, long before we did. But when I heard King, I thought, Ah-ha. One of us has finally learned what the white man has known all along. Say the word *God* and thousands, perhaps millions, will follow in whatever direction we point. That made him dangerous. But it made me also wonder if he was cunning. Because if he was he'd position himself to be perceived as only a nuisance until it was too late to stop him. But if he was sincere, he'd present himself as a threat. And we all know the fate of those who choose to become threats: This society has no place for you.

Cunning is the wire what picks the lock and lets us into the house and at the family jewels.

King didn't love me. King loved King. And maybe his

family, friends, and associates. And to me that is proper. I love me, I love my life and want to partake in the maximum of what life has to offer. Therefore I had to be cunning. I had to play both sides of the street. I lived in the Village and worked at a college where my colleagues and friends, most all of them white, supported and respected me. Because I was black all of them assumed that I was passionately caught up and moved by all that was going on in the streets of Alabama, Mississippi, and Birmingham, when the honest-to-God truth is that I didn't really give a damn. I watched the news reports, read the papers, and thought, What a shame, but that was it. Those people getting their heads busted or split open had nothing to do with me. The only thing we had in common was color. And anybody who thought that I would be foolish enough to expose my body and mind to that kind of abuse didn't really know me at all. I have too much love for this head, these arms, this torso, and these legs to risk any form of injury to them—in the holy name of anything, be it religion, civil rights, or the other great magic word, *democracy*. I wasn't that dumb, and never have been. Only thing is, people expect you to be, so I learned very early on to maintain various poses.

Uptown I acted pissed off and outraged about what was going on. Downtown, I acted upset and deeply wounded. White male colleagues would actually apologize to me about what was going on. And I would humbly accept those apologies, telling them softly, "I understand." But with the women it seemed to work like poetry. All these beautiful creatures, sometimes shimmeringly so, would look me in the eye, searching for the hurt, and when they found it would touch my cheek softly and tell me, "I know it's difficult, but things are going to change for the better. Believe me." Often they would prove it by accompanying me to bed. And I began to think, Hey, there's something to be gained by all that rallying in the streets. If I picked my spots carefully, avoided areas of maximum danger, and take up positions close to where TV cameras might spot me—who knows what a boon that could be to my social and sensual life. But at the moment there was one thing wrong. I was clean faced. So the first item on the agenda was—to grow a beard.

In Violence We Trust

Joanie, late twenties

America is a violent land. A society forged out of violence and deeply in need of violence to maintain our identity. I didn't know Martin King, but I loved him. I had followed his activities, read his books, contributed money to his cause, and wrote letters of protest when he was imprisoned. I remember feeling anger and humiliation when he was spat upon and called names like Troublemaker, Nigger, and Communist, and by some of our elected officials.

Didn't we know what we were doing? Didn't we know that this was a great man passing through our midsts? . . . I recall a speech I made to my class one day, saying in effect that from time to time we are visited by greatness. Or have "greatness" thrust upon us. That great men exist right now and right here. But we're so used to reading about them in history books we refuse to believe or accept that they could be living in our country and in our time. "In India maybe or the Far East, perhaps. But here, in America? Give me a break." . . . My seventh graders of course didn't understand what I was talking about. But I was talking about him. About Martin Luther King Jr. The man America killed because it was threatened by his greatness.

They said he was standing on a balcony when the fatal shot was fired. What he was doing there has never been satisfactorily explained. They said he was out there taking the air. That's reasonable enough. Innocent enough, unless you're a black man trying to better the condition of your people in America. Then you're embarking on a dangerous interlude.

For white America doesn't want her darker brethren reaching after equality. She wants things to remain the same. Forever and ever the same. And anything or anyone who comes along and tries to change that pattern makes her angry. Very angry. Violently angry. And that's when the bullets fly. We can never be sure about anything. Never be confident about anything until we let the bullets fly. Then we're happy. Then we're fine. Then we're American, once again. The only problem is: Somebody has to pay the price. First it was him. But one day it's sure to be—you.

The Trainer

Louie, forties, dressed in a sweat suit

Alright, here we go. Hit it, hit it, hit it! Get a rhythm going, that's what you got to do. Hit it, move . . . hit it move. Don't ever be a stationary target. Hit, move, shift, hook, slide then hook again. Now don't forget about the jab. Everything flows off the jab. But you got to be in position to throw it. Stop what you doing and watch me for a minute.

He demonstrates throwing the jab. First fast, then in slow motion, then fast again.

It's like an electric current starting at the back of your heel and ending up on the edge of your fist. You learn to throw the jab right and nobody'll get near you. But you can't be a stationary target. Stick and move, stick and move, all the time. And when you throw you got to do it all together. Can't just throw one out. Got to be in numbers. Combinations, combinations, combinations. Bip, bip, bip . . . One, two, three. Bip, bip, bip, bip. One two three four. Bip, bip, bip, bip, bip. One two three four five. It all got to come together. All got to be by the numbers. *(Stops moving around)* Keep going, don't stop just because I stop.

My brother, boy. If he had just listened to me, everything woulda been fine. He had it. Had it all. Speed, strength, and a tough hard body. Put that combination together with discipline, training, and skill and we coulda gone straight to the top. Straight to the top in his division. I told him so. He said, "Yeah, yeah," but he wasn't listening. Or if he was, he wasn't believing. See, a man got to believe he can make something happen, then he can get the incentive to work for it. My brother didn't believe so he just didn't work. Now he's just another clown out there talking about all the things he coulda done, and all the opportunities he was denied. Don't you believe any of it. I tried to show that boy. Even sent him the money to come to the city. Told him when he got here, "This is a place of temptation. This is Sodom and Gomorrah. But it don't have to be if a man keep his head on his shoulders and his eye on the goal." I couldn't do it no more. My eyes had gone bad. Couldn't see the punches coming to get out of the way. But I had the skills. Everybody know I had the skills. All I had to do was teach them to my brother and we would be a winning combination. But he didn't want to hear it. He wanted the glory but didn't want the pain. Told me that he didn't like getting hit. I told him, "This is boxing. You got to get hit sometime." But he didn't want to know. Just want to go in there, knock folks out, and go home untouched with all them women smiling at him telling him how pretty he look in there. And for a while he was doing it until one night. The referee counted him out and that was that. He quit. Couldn't get him to go near a gym ever again.

He broke my heart, I'll tell you. I had plans for him. Plans for myself, too. . . . But what the hell. Life goes on, right? Now it's your turn. You can be the man if you want to be. But it got to be for you. Can't be for anybody else. Not for me or your mother or your father or your girlfriend. You got to want it for yourself. And you got to work for it. Ain't nobody gon' come down and give you no gift. Work, work, work, train, train, train, that's the name of this game.

But if you want it you can have it. That's what I told my brother and that's what I'm telling you. You both have the same talent, the same kind of skills. The rest is up to you.

Now let's start all over again, see if you remember all the things I showed you. As I call the numbers let me see your combinations. 1 – 2 – 3 . . . 1 – 2 – 3 – 4 – 5 . . . 3 – 2 – 1 . . . 4 – 3 – 1 – 2 – 2 – 1 – 4 . . . yeah, yeah. Coming good. I like what I see more every day. . . . Take a break catch your breath, drink some water. We'll start again in ten minutes.

Sunday Morning Memories

Cynthia, early thirties

Sunday mornings we used to lie there sometimes all day. It would start in the morning, move to the afternoon, and want to move into the night, but I had to leave which is the only reason we stopped.

I would get to his place 'round eight thirty or nine, knock, and the door would open up. He would be standing there naked or sometimes just in his shorts and that thing would be standing straight out like a rock. And I would say, "Boy, what you doing opening the door like that?" And he would just answer, "I been thinking 'bout you and waiting for you to get here." And sometimes to tease him or just to be mean I would say, "What if it wasn't me that knocked on the door? . . . What if Louie didn't let me come out this morning? . . . What if I couldn't get away? What would you do with that thing standing out straight like that?" He wouldn't answer. He would just come real close and I could tell by the way he was breathing that his heart was beating fast. And he would move hisself against me and I would have to tell him to be careful not to make a mess of my dress.

"Then take it off," he would say, still short of breath.

"But I just got here."

"Take it off, come on. Here I'll help you."

But I used to fight it just a little bit because it was less than an hour before that I went to all that trouble to make myself pretty to go over there. But he didn't care. He want me how he want me and that was naked on the bed with him flat on top of me. And it ain't that I didn't want that, too. It's just that I thought we should talk a little bit first. Listen to gospel music on the radio. Think about them church bells singing in the background. I grew up with gospel music and church bells. And that's what Sunday mornings used to mean to me until he came along and changed all that.

Now Sunday mornings meant going up to his little room and taking all my clothes off. He would kiss me in places I ain't never been kissed before and I would kiss him right back all over. I was a married woman but I wasn't getting this kind of attention at home. Louie wasn't bad but he just didn't have that kind of imagination.

With Josh, things would start one way, change into something else, and then start all over again. Once we got into it there wasn't time for much conversation. Or for me to worry that parts of my clothes was on one side of the room while the rest was somewhere else.

Josh had energy to spare. I had to be the only woman he was seeing because I could sense he was saving it all up for these Sunday mornings.

We never talked about love or feelings because I didn't want to spoil it. I was a married woman with a husband and a child. He was a single man living in the city that didn't know too many people. He was lonely I could tell and I was doing what I could to help. But I could only do so much. I had duties at home.

One day he asked if I ever thought about leaving my husband. And I told him the truth—no. He smiled a little smile and never asked the question again.

We went on like that for more than a year. If Louie had any idea about what was going on he never gave a clue. It was like living in a dream world. During the week I had one kind of existence, and every Sunday morning it was a whole different ball game.

Sometimes by myself I would think about the future

and ask myself: "How long you planning on keeping this thing going?" And the child in me would answer, "Forever and ever." But nothing lasts forever and I knew some day it would have to end. What I wasn't prepared for was when and how.

One Sunday morning I got dressed as usual, took the train, and went to that derelict building he lived in. Walked up the stairs and knocked on the door. No answer. Knocked on the door some more. Still no answer. I thought maybe he went out. So I waited and periodically kept on knocking. Finally the super came up and asked what I was doing. Told him I was waiting for Josh.

"Well you gon' be waiting a long time," he said. "That man moved out in the middle of the week."

"Did he say why or give any forwarding address?"

"Nope. Just gave me the keys and said he'd be leaving. The room is empty. If you don't believe me I could get the keys and show it to you."

"I believe you," I told him and left. Couldn't go back home. Louie would've wanted to know how come I was back so soon. Far as he knew I had gone to church and would be visiting with my grandmother like I do every Sunday.

So I walked the streets of the neighborhood looking at faces thinking I might see Josh. Then I went into a bar, ordered a beer, and told myself that he would drop me a line or give me a call. He wouldn't just disappear in the atmosphere like that. Not after all the things we'd done and all the things we'd meant to each other. No, he'd have to come back. We'd have to reconnect.

But that was a lie. It's been four years now and I'm beginning to wonder if he even was real. I don't have a picture or a memento to say, "This was from Josh. He really did exist."

Louie is the same, only a little bit older. I'm the same, too, only a little bit sadder. I had it here, right here in my hands, and I let it get away.

Now on Sunday mornings I really go to church and hear the bells ringing. I sing and I even say prayers. But every so often I stop and pause and I remember with a smile how it used to be once—a long, long time ago.

The Lottery Winner

Sophie, late fifties

Money is something I ain't ever been excited about. Ain't ever had any—so it stands to reason that you can't get excited about what you never had.

Now when I won that lottery for some reason it seem like my whole life change. Six million dollars to be paid out to me over the next twenty years. Isn't that something? Six mil . . . To tell the truth I don't even know why I bought the ticket. I ain't a gambling woman. And I ain't no dreamer either. I guess I was feeling sorry for Old Blind George on the corner selling them newspapers. He been there for twenty years and nothing don't ever seem to change for him. So that morning when I pass to get my paper as usual and he said, "What about a lottery ticket, too, Miss Johnson, you never know. Might change your luck. Can't win if you don't play." Now he say that all the time and I always say, "No thanks. Not for me today." But this time I said "Why not?" and bought one. Now I'm a millionaire, or that's what they tell me.

It didn't change anything . . . or shouldn't have. I still live in the same place, go to the same job. Only now everything's different. The day after it was announced in the paper my boss and all the people down on the job had a special luncheon for me. I didn't know why. "Just to celebrate the fact that you been so long here with us," they said. I had no idea they had even noticed or cared.

Family and friends I ain't seen for years start calling up and dropping by. "Why? What's the occasion?" "No reason," they would say, "Just want to see how you is doing. That's all."

"I'm doing fine," I tell them, "real fine." "What you planning to do with it?" they always ask. "Don't know yet."

"Well, keep us in mind. Maybe we got some ideas you might want to hear." Others sit and go over old times telling me how much I mean to them and how much they think about me all the time.

The funniest ones is the men who try to date me. I been single for nearly fifteen years since my husband died. In all that time I've had me about five dates and all of them were jokes. Now they were ringing my phone so much that I had to have the number changed and unlisted. Everybody want to take me dancing, or on a boat ride, or to the movies. And they come in all ages, too. From the half-cripple old man who live upstairs to the young bus driver who live down the block. Sometimes they meet me in front of the building on my way to work and want to walk me to the train station. I look in the mirror to see what's the change but I didn't get any prettier or younger. So it could only be one thing them folks is after. And one thing alone *(Spelling it)* M-O-N-E-Y.

Winning that money can be a blessing or a curse. I'm determined to make it a blessing. The first thing I plan to do when I get that first check is split it down the middle between me and Old Blind George. If he want to quit selling newspapers and change his life, he'll have the means. Then with the rest of it I'm planning to spread it equally to the church, some schools, three places for the homeless, and that place they have for training handicapped children. They'll make good use of the money. I know that.

When I first heard the news I thought I would spread it out equally among all my family and friends. But now that I see what the idea of money is doing to their character I can't contribute to that. They ain't gon' like me for it, but I'm helping them in ways they will never understand. Ain't that so?

Hate

Barney, thirties

I just got back from a funeral. The funeral of a man I've hated all my life. A man I promised to kill. But not just like that. *(Snaps his finger)* Nooo—I intended to make him suffer for a long time and then die. I wanted to make him cry, make him repent, make him regret the wrong that he had done, and then die. But it wasn't to be. Old age, alcohol, loneliness, and cancer did the job before I could get to him. And from what I hear, I guess they did the job much better than I ever could, even in my wildest dream.

What did this man do to me that I could hate him so much you ask. Well, it's simple. He killed my mother. I didn't know her well. Didn't know her well at all. I was only six when he did the deed. The story went like this. Two years after I was born my father and mother were divorced. He took off somewhere in the cosmos and was never seen or heard of again. My mother, who worked as nurse, met up with this man Gabriel whom she had known ever since they were youngsters. Apparently he had a crush on her carried forward from all those years. Now he in his early thirties and she in her late twenties met up again and solidified that relationship that had started so long ago. They lived together for more than a year and the plan was for them to be married. He was even going to adopt me and give me his name. But then things started to go wrong. He apparently drank a lot and she didn't like it. There were fights, he would beat her, and the whole fabric of the relationship began to unravel. She moved out on him and started seeing another man. One early morning he went to where she was staying. They got into an argument, he pulled a gun and shot her dead. Simple, short, and complete as that. (*Pause*)

Where was I while all this was going on? In the other room asleep. I heard the gunshot noise, I remember, and then a lot of people moving around the house. They wouldn't let me see. I remember the police and the flashing lights. But that's about all.

Gabriel was found guilty of manslaughter, not murder. He was sentenced to seven years and was released on parole after four and a half. He returned to the town as a hero of sorts. A man who didn't allow "no woman to make a fool of him by going with another man while he still had his claim on her." Word was that the other man was lucky he didn't catch a bullet, too. And by the time Gabriel got out of jail that man was long gone.

Gabriel went back to work, picked up with another woman, got married, and had three children.

I was my mother's only child. And she didn't have any other family but an older sister. So that's where I was sent to live. I think that woman beat me from the first day I moved in until the day I ran away when I felt I couldn't take it anymore. I think she was mean mostly out of frustration because she didn't have a man and people said she was ugly.

I remember my mother as a gentle soul and I used to dream about her all the time.

I was gone for more than a week before the authorities caught me. They took me back to my aunt but she said she couldn't handle me. So I was sent from one foster home to another. Some good, some bad. . . . I don't even want to talk about it.

Somehow I grew up, went to school, and even got my degree. But I never forgot that man Gabriel. And what he did to my mother and me. In my quiet hours I would scheme and plan and walk through all kinds of scenarios for exacting my revenge.

When I couldn't take fantasizing any longer, I moved back to the town. More than twenty years had passed. Nobody knew who I was. Things had changed but Gabriel was still there. He was old now and all by himself. His wife had died and his children had come to no good. One was in jail, one was somewhere in Philly running with a bad crowd, they said. And the girl, Joanie, was some kind of drug head working as a waitress in Miami.

Gabriel lived in a broken-down old house and drank from the time he woke up in the morning until he passed out at night.

I went to visit him once. He had no idea who I was. Told him I was a friend of his son, Bobby. We sat for an hour and talked about things. He didn't make much sense. All he did was drink. I asked him about my mother. He couldn't remember much. He mumbled something about "a whoring bitch" and gulped some more whiskey. I didn't know what to do. I wanted to kill him, but suddenly I also wanted to leave. It was as though this great distance had come between us even though I was sitting not more than six or seven feet from him.

I left and went back home. But kept in touch with what was going on. When I heard he had died I flew back for the funeral. It was a sorry affair really. Fifteen people if there were that many. None of his children were present, of course. The minister said some kind words and we all dispersed. I went to a bar, sat for a few hours drinking beer and thinking. Then I left, came back to the hotel and thought some more. Humph. You carry a thing around with you so long it becomes hard to let go. And that's where I'm at now. The man is dead. He's gone, but the hate just won't let me go. It sits here on my shoulders and here in my chest. It presses me down, squeezes me inside, and refuses to evaporate. I don't know what to do. So I'm asking you, whoever you are to help me. I need it. I need it real bad.

Dream Lover: Mr. Blues

April, thirties

There's this man I always dream about. My fantasy figure you might say. He is a music playing man who blows the horns of Orpheus and the pipes of Pan. Who would stand in a corner playing the music of now but quickly and without any warning take you all the way back to Buddy Bolden and beyond. He and his music will take me past the sadness and the pain back to the sweetness and the sweet pleasure that used to be there in the night when you could put away all the ambitions and concerns of the day and deal with the matter at hand: me in his arms and him in mine.

Lovers come and go, but fantasies stay and improve and get perfect and more perfect with each passing day, if you nurture them properly.

"I love you," he would say.

"I need you," I would explain.

"Let's make love," he would tell me. And "How do you want it?" would be my reply.

The trouble with love is that it doesn't last. It is a perishable commodity. A fruit that must be eaten when it was ripe and sweet. Or else it will soften and rot and then one day turn rancid and stink. I'm not telling you what I've read about or heard. I'm telling you what I've made the mistake of living too many times, on too many nights, in too many beds. Sometimes it was their fault, other times it was mine. Makes no nevermind anyhow, there are still lessons to be learned and dreams to be fulfilled. And that's when Blues Lover came to my rescue, whispering in my ear, dancing in my heart: And blowing in my mind.

He used to be a composite of all the men that passed over and through me. Especially you and you and you and you. But now his features are all his own. From the curly crop of hair that covers his scalp and brain, to that little brown rosebud below his waist that elongates and comes to life when I walk into view, with or without any clothes on.

On the street he never looks at other women or tells me I'm getting fat. In bars he doesn't get drunk or insulting. And what moods he has are just the ones I need for the mood I'm in at the moment . . . Love is a given. And sex is a canoe ride down a wild river full of danger, excitement, adventure, and risk that always gets me home safely at the end. *(Pause)*

In your letter *(She looks at the letter)* you ask if you could come back. If I could forgive and forget and we could start all over again. You said you learned your lesson. Well, I've learned mine, too. And the simple truth is the place would be too crowded with you and my phantom lover, too. He comes when I call him, stays as long as I need him, and only leaves when I feel like being alone. He is the soul that keeps me standing, the music that keeps me going, and the spirit that sees me through. I'm sorry, old boy, there's just no room for you anymore. This lady is spoken for.

You Can't Win for Losing

Preston, forties

Well, anyway I said to the man, "I'm a lawyer not a magician, I'll do the best I can but it's got to be honorable. I'm not going to throw myself at the mercy of the court on your behalf, or try any tricks that might be considered cheap or undignified. I hope you understand that." He said he did. Then I explained that statutory rape was a serious offense. He claimed he understood but didn't feel he was guilty. "Sure the girl was underage, but I didn't force her into anything. We were lovers by mutual consent. It's her parents who are having trouble with this, not she or I."

"Yes. But it's also her parents who have brought charges against you, so their opinion is what matters, not hers." He said he understood but yet insisted that I enter a "not guilty" plea. I advised against it, but he insisted.

When we walked into court I knew that there'd be trouble. Moments after the judge heard the plea he called the DA and myself into chambers.

"What's the meaning of this 'not guilty' plea?" he asked. "Your Honor, my client feels that based on the particular nature of this case, he is not guilty." "Did penetration take place?" the judge asked. "Yes, but—" "I'll ask you again, did penetration take place?" "Yes, your Honor." "And your client admits that?" "Yes—but with the young lady's consent. They were lovers."

"Doesn't matter. Once penetration occurs and the girl is underage that constitutes rape, statutory rape under the definition of the law. Now either you change your plea to 'guilty' or I won't hear the case."

I went out and told my client we had to change the plea. "But I'll have a record if you do," he said.

"He won't hear the case if we don't and possibly face worse consequences with the next judge we face. This city may be big but these judges talk to each other. The dispensing of justice isn't as impartial as we're often led to believe it is. You're a black man involved with a white girl; that's not going to help your case."

He let me change the plea but he wasn't happy. I argued his case and he got off with a two-year suspended sentence. I thought I did good but apparently he didn't. Because now he's telling people that I'm a crummy lawyer and that I sold him down the river. Worse than that, he's refusing to pay me the last third of my fee. He says I didn't earn it. Says that if he had represented himself he would've gotten the same result.

What I wish is that he had represented himself. Then he might've had some understanding as to what we lawyers do.

You can't win in this profession so I guess there's no point in complaining. But every so often somebody really gets to you. This guy did.

The Cellist

Renee, late twenties, is a cellist. She has her instrument with her; she plays a few chords, then speaks.

I came from a family of eight. All girls. My mother taught English at a junior high and played concert piano. Father ran a detox center until the day he became so depressed at witnessing all that human misery that he took to drinking himself. After that it was a short trip to fooling with girls half his age and the breakup of our family via divorce.

But before that he made sure we were all on our way to a solid *liberal* education. And that we were all trained in the arts. I was going to the theatre at six, reading adult novels at nine. And I learned to play the cello at twelve. By the time I was thirteen, I was playing my first local concert.

I learned very early on looking at derelicts searching through garbage on the streets that "There but for the grace of God go I."

"All men are created equal in the sight of God." At school we were always being divided up—blacks and whites. But I never felt comfortable with it so I would seek out white girls to befriend. They weren't easy to know, but I was determined not to be a bigot. When they did accept me into their group I was ostracized by some of my black friends. I never meant for that to happen. I just wanted friends on both sides. But like it or not, I was told I had to choose.

After Dad left, Mother had a white boyfriend for a while. He was a musician, too. Played the piano. Often I'd see him looking at me, but I didn't exactly know why. Sometimes at night we could hear Mom and he in the bedroom after they thought we'd gone to sleep. There'd be moans and cries and great sighs of satisfaction. One night Mom spoke out about something quite explicit, in a moment of ecstasy, I suppose. It made my sister, Karen, and I blush and slink away from the door where we'd been listening. We never talked about it afterwards, or hid by the door again. *(Pause)*

His name was Lee, the piano man. Clean, well-groomed and well-spoken. One day he said to me, quite seriously, "You know, you're very pretty. If the law didn't forbid it, I would take you into that bedroom instead of your mother." I was sixteen years old and he talked to me that way.

I never told Mom about this conversation but I avoided Lee whenever I could. Some months later she broke up with him. When I asked her why, she said it wasn't working out. Then she said the oddest thing to me. She said, "If you want him, you can have him—I'm finished with him for good." I never understood why she said that. And I still don't.

She goes back to her instrument and continues playing.

The Magician

Wilson, mid fifties

Lookie here. You sit up on the stoop like this every day and after a while it get so that you seen everything in life. Everything. I've seen people born, grow up, go off, get rich, change their life, and come back here for a visit with their nose in the air, like this neighborhood ain't never had nothing to do with them. Then there are others you couldn't get outta this place if you had a gun. Some of them shoulda left for their own good. But maybe they wasn't brave enough. Or didn't know that there's a bigger world out there waiting.

Anyway, a cat I just seen put me in mind of a man that used to live and operate in these parts. He ain't no more but for a good while he was a man folk on this block used to pay a lot of attention to. Name was McKenzie. Algernon McKenzie. People used to call him Professor Algie. Man was a pimp. But he do his business in such a way that people used to look at him like he was involved in a respectable profession. Yes, Professor Algie was smart and cool. Cool as anybody I ever know or seen in the movies. Yes sir, that man was something and a half. Dress well, talk well.

And he had an eye for talent, too. That was his strong point. He would take the ugliest, shabbiest, plainest-looking loser on the block and add her to his stable. And all us street boys would wonder why.

But the Professor always had a plan. And before he turned them out for business he would take them under his wing and school them. Nobody exactly know what he did or how he did it. And none of the girls ever tell. But after

Professor Algie finished with them, they would be some of the sweetest, hottest, finest foxes money could buy.

After a while we started calling him "The Magician" 'cause we figured he could do magic with women. Guys I know used to bring him their wives, girlfriends, and sisters just to see if he could bring out what was hiding inside them.

The Professor got to be so popular and well known he started wearing dark clothes and a cape, carrying a cane waving it at folks saying, "This is my magic wand." We all thought it was a joke, but a lot of people said Professor Algie was serious. Cat really believe he was some kind of special magician. Still it was fun watching him walking around, waving his wand—whatever he believed.

Well, I'm sorry to say he came to a bad end. Sorry because I used to enjoy watching him on the street. Man had style, a whole lot of style. But all that came to an end one day just like that. *(Snaps his fingers)* A police bullet put a stop to the show and that was all she wrote . . . Apparently he got into a fight with a cop. Black cop— don't know what the fight was all about. Nobody ever told me. Anyhow, they say he raised his hand with the cane, maybe to put his magic spell on the man, but I guess the cop thought he was going to hit him. So the cop put his pistol right on Algie's chest and pulled the trigger. Pow! Blowed his whole back away, cape and everything. Pow! . . .

I wasn't there but folks told me he had this surprised expression on his face. Like he wasn't supposed to die or something. I guess it was like the fellows said, he really did believe all that foolishness about being a magician. I woulda swear Professor Algie knew better, would swear it on a stack of Bibles, and woulda even bet my paycheck on it. But then again, I would been wrong. Woulda been real wrong. So you see it just goes to show you, even I don't know everything. I know a whole lotta stuff, but I don't know everything. And you know what that is? It's a shame. A real damn shame.

Some Men

Laurie, mid twenties

I said no because I really wasn't in the mood. All I wanted to do was go home, go to sleep, and wake up the next day. That's all I wanted, but he kept on insisting. Saying that if I didn't I'd be putting a damper on what had been a nearly perfect evening. I don't know about perfect, but the evening had been fun and he had spent a lot of money. And he had been real nice. So I said, "Yes," because—well—it seemed to mean so much to him. Men get like that sometimes. So what do you do? You give in. Not because you want to, but because— well, it's easier, that's all. Just a lot easier. So he touched me and we kissed. Then he asked if I would let him undress me. Some older men like to do that, so I said, "Sure. Why not?" So I just stood there and he did.

When it was over he asked if I would stay the night. Again I said, "Sure." I mean, I was already naked and in bed. So why not? Besides, who wants to hassle out on the street for a cab that late at night? This is a strange city. You never know what kinds of creatures will come wandering out of the shadows while you're standing there waving your hand. So I stayed the night.

The next morning he wanted to again. So I let him get on top of me. He tried and tried. I could feel his heart beating, but it just wasn't happening. I don't know why. I did what I could to help, but it wasn't meant to be. There just wasn't any life down there and that's how it was. Last night there had been; today there wasn't. What can you do? You give up, that's all. It just mean that it wasn't meant to be. He tried some more but it only made matters worse. So finally I said, "Look, this isn't going to happen. I think we better forget it." He agreed and got out of the bed. When he came back he was completely dressed but his attitude was different.

"I think you better leave," he said. "I think you better get the hell out." I said, "Sure." Then he started saying that the reason he couldn't do it was because I was a whore and a dog. I couldn't understand why he was talking to me like this. "I was nice to you," I told him. "I was nice to you for a whole night. Why can't you be nice to me in return?" But he wasn't listening. All he kept saying was, "Get out. Get out before I do something to you that I'll regret." And I believed him, too. There was something about his face and his eyes that told me to get out of there in a hurry. And I did, too. I got out of there fast. Real fast. So fast that I was still fixing my clothes while I was walking on the street.

Jesus! Jesus! Can you believe that? He couldn't get it up so it was my fault. Figure that one out. Boy, people in this city can be strange sometimes. Real strange. And the problem is, you can't spot it. They look like everybody else until it's too late. Too damn late. I hate people, you know that. I hate everybody in the whole damn world. I hate everybody so much that you know what I sometimes think about doing?

I think about swimming. Way, way out. So far that nobody could ever see me or find me again. That's right, I would be gone. Gone with the waves. . . . The way I would do it is simple. I would walk out in the ocean all the way to where I couldn't touch bottom, then putting one hand in front of the other I would begin swimming, moving further and further out to sea, but never looking back and never stopping to catch my breath. . . . I'd swim to the horizon, then to the horizon after that and then to the one way, way beyond that. The sea would never end and I would just keep going and going, and going some more. Then guess what? I'd be back to where I started. Back to the land. Only thing is, it would all be different. Oh the trees and the beach, the sand and even the water would all be the same. But the people would be different. That's right, the people. And I would be different, too. Don't ask me how because I'm not sure. I just know I would be different, and that would be fine. More than fine, that would be great. Just great.

The Evangelist

Yannis, late thirties, carrying a Bible or prayer book

The world is a dangerous place to live in, my friends. And if you don't believe me, take a look at the stories in the newspapers and on TV. Listen to the gossip of your friends and loved ones. Stand on any street corner in any big city for more than a half hour and you're sure to see something sinful, evil, and sad. You may even know a victim of one of these events, or may have been a victim yourself.

The world is a dangerous, frightening, and deadly place. Looking around we see plane crashes, train wrecks, car accidents, bank robberies, mass suicides and war, drunkenness, drug addiction, adultery, fornication, and greed. All of these and more are some of the dangers that surround us daily and come to visit us when we least expect it.

Is there any place of safety, or escape from all these evils, you may ask. And the cynic will tell you "No, the world is all around and there's nothing you can do to escape it." But that's not really true. Because God, the Father in Heaven, the Maker of the Universe, which includes this tortured planet, has provided safety for you. Safety and escape. But only if you want it. You've got to want it and seek it out. *(Pause)*

The night was dark and cold. A wind came down from the mountains freezing our bones. In less than an hour a white sheet of snow covered the ground. The men wanted to bed down for the night. But I refused their request, because I knew the enemy would be doing the same thing. Covering up and hiding from the brute force of the weather. So we marched forward into the storm, bending our bodies, but clutching to our weapons. When we got within range I sent scouts ahead to check their positions. When they returned we adjusted our artillery and opened fire like it was the end of the world. The skies lit up and shadows kept bouncing in every direction. One moment it was a cold, blistering night, and the next it was the Fourth of July. The following morning when we added up the tally, there was over a hundred dead, without any loss of men on our side. We had done our job well. We had destroyed the enemy with proficiency and speed, with grit, cunning and know-how. Utilizing the military man's greatest single weapon—the element of surprise. We had been trained and we'd learned our lesson well. We had become killers of men.

Today I want to train you in a different art. I want to make you *Saviors of Men.* Let us pray.

The Living Symbol

Fletcher, forties, is blind

HELP ME. PLEASE HELP ME. THE WAYS OF THE
FLESH ARE GONE FROM MY LIFE. ALL I'VE GOT IS
MEMORIES FROM A LONG AGO DREAM. AND THE
LIGHT OF THE LORD TO SHOW ME THE WAY.
EVERYTHING ELSE IS DARKNESS. ONLY DARK-
NESS. BUT JESUS IS THE LIGHT . . . I LOVE JESUS
AND BEG FOR HIS FORGIVENESS. I SEEK FORGIVE-
NESS FOR MY SINS AND THE SINS OF THE
WORLD. PLEASE. PLEASE GIVE TO THE POOR AND
DOWNTRODDEN WHO'VE DONE NOTHING
MORE THAN TO BE BORN ON A PLANET WITH SO
MUCH SUFFERING AND PAIN . . . THE LORD WILL
BLESS YOU FOR IT. SO PLEASE, PLEASE GIVE. *(Pause)*
    Today I heard a man on the street, a derelict, I suppose,
shouting to everyone passing by: "HEY EVERYBODY! . . .
LISTEN UP! AND LISTEN UP REAL GOOD. I AIN'T
BEEN LAID IN EIGHT YEARS. THAT'S RIGHT, YOU
HEARD THE NUMBER—EIGHT YEARS! AND YOU
WANT TO KNOW SOMETHING? I DON'T CARE. IT
DON'T BOTHER ME. AND I'LL TELL YOU WHY. I
AM AT PEACE WITH MYSELF AND I AM AT PEACE
WITH THE WORLD. SO I DON'T NEED LOVE OF
ANY KIND." . . . That's what the man kept saying over and
over again. That he was at peace with the world. Well, so am
I. Maybe I don't look it, but I am totally at peace.
    I fought for this country, gave up my sight for it, and
never got anything in return except for a jive check that come

in once a month, which just about covers the rent for that little hole I live in. The rest of what I need to keep body and soul together, I get from you kind people out here on the streets. That's right and that's the truth.

I am the symbol, the living symbol of the black man's freedom realized. A symbol of all the lies they tell you, and all the truths that you can't escape. I am the American dream . . . Or did I say scream? . . . No, I said dream. That's right, you heard it right . . . Dream.

Us

Jamila, mid twenties

You know what I dream about? Us. Us living in a town far, far away from here. Some little town where the houses have fireplaces and narrow little country roads where you could walk for hours and hours and see only trees and flowers. Or maybe a horse or a cow or a windmill or just a stack of hay. I want us to go some place where you could have a job doing something you like. And we could have a nice little house with a basement and an attic, maybe.

Wouldn't that be great? Wouldn't that just be the best? And we could have it too, honey. It doesn't just have to be a dream. Other people have it, why can't we? But you have to be patient. You got to hold your temper. I know it hard. I know that people mess with you and you ain't never been one to back down from a fight. But every time you get into a scene they add more days and weeks to your time. And the longer you in here, the longer I'm going to be out here waiting. It's like both of us are in prison. You in there, me out there. So try to be good, please. If not for yourself, for us. Okay?

Silent No More

Harris, late twenties

I agreed to going on that TV talk show because I think it's about time one of us talked back. Black brothers, I mean. Man, if you listen to all the stuff you hear about us on them shows and believe what they write about us in magazines, then you got to think that the black man is maybe the worst species of human being God ever created. Because besides all the criminal things they tell you we done and continue to do, they also tell you that we lazy, low-minded, drunk or drugged up most of the time, and that we don't know how to treat our women. More than we don't know how to treat them, we don't even know how to see any beauty in them. You see we all walking around blind except when some white woman pass our way, I guess. I don't know. But that's what they put in the magazines. And on TV. And I'm not just talking about white people either. I'm talking about our black sisters. Some of them anyway. They the ones you see on them talk shows talking about what bad role models we are. And what a shame that is. And one that I was watching the other day, she jumped up in front of the camera and said: "Let's talk it plain, black men are dogs!" Man, the whole audience just clap their hands and shout back to her, "That's right, Sister! You telling the truth. They is dogs, every one of them!" . . . And I sat there thinking, I ain't no dog. And I don't appreciate nobody calling me one. Especially on TV. If somebody had say that to my face I would knock them down. I don't care how big they are, or how small. I grew up respecting women and I expect them to respect me, too. My mother was a woman and I respected her. When I got to a certain age, she respected me, too. That's the way I think things should be. "Do unto others as you would have them do unto you" is the rule I grew up with. And I try to live by it. But it don't seem like too many people go by that any more. Especially when they get on TV. It's like that camera give them a license to curse you, insult you, and call you any bad name they wish. And you, 'cause you're a man, ain't supposed to say nothing about it. You supposed to take it quietly and keep your mouth shut. I mean, those people assassinating your character to a million or maybe ten million people and you ain't supposed to say a damn thing except to agree. And maybe stand up in front of everybody like they do at AA meetings and say, "My name is So-and-So. I am a black man; therefore, I am a dog." I don't think so. And I ain't doing it. Hell, no. In fact I'm doing just the opposite. I'm going on that TV show and let the world hear my side of things. And when I do, I ain't gon' be speaking for every black man. I'm going to be speaking just for me. The rest of them don't want to talk, that's their business. I know for me, I just don't want to be silent no more.

MOODY'S MOOD CAFÉ

Moody's Mood Café is an actual place, but it is also a state of mind. It was named after King Pleasure's "Moody's Mood for Love" and the sound of that tune seems to echo in the background always.

This is a place where the lonely, the wounded, and the lost come to sit, drink, and meditate in silence. And as they look out at the world with pained, haunted eyes, we hear their thoughts and sense their confusion.

This Business

Nunez, late thirties, the bartender

This business is about losers. Absolute losers. These people come in here sit, drink, and stare at the walls. When they get tired they pay, leave, and go someplace else where they do the same thing. All over again. Some of them got jobs so they come in early, take a few gulps, and then go off. Later in the evening I see them again. And we don't have to talk much. I know what they want, so I set it up, they drink it and pay.

People like Wilson and Jimmy over there, I got them all day, morning into the night. Lucky me. . . . Used to have a monsignor from the church around the corner. One of the few black monsignors in the Catholic Church they tell me. Cat was old, but he sure liked his Johnny Walker Black. Used to say it was "the staff of his life" and "the elixir of his spirit." Had a bottle on the table next to his bed, he told me. So it was the last thing he'd see at night before going to sleep. And when he woke up the following morning, the first thing he'd do is pour himself a shot. Before saying his prayers, before brushing his teeth. First thing he'd taste was that sweet golden water.

Pours himself a drink, sips it for a bit, then continues talking.

Like to sit right here at the bar and talk about his problems with the church. All the priests he had to manage but couldn't. And all the nuns he said who should go out and get laid. "That's all they need," he would say, "just a little bit of flesh on their flesh. Then they wouldn't be giving me so much grief."

45

He was a funny dude. Like to tell a lot of dirty jokes, too. But sometimes he'd talk serious. Said the Catholic Church wasn't a religion for black folks. Said it was too quiet and subdued. We need places where we could get all emotional and yell. Where we could let the spirit hold us and take us out of ourselves. "The Catholic Church doesn't provide that kind of outlet. That's why it can't serve the needs of our black parishioners." That's what the man used to say. Now, I'm not religious, so I don't know. But that's what he used to say while sitting here drinking up all that booze. Was a good tipper, too. Five dollars on a twenty-dollar check. Ten dollars on a thirty. We don't get many like that in here. No sir. Not at this bar. What we get is those who want you to give them a free drink after every third or fourth one they buy, and we do it. What the hell, it's only liquor. But, he was a nice change *(Sips his drink some more)*. . . . One day I come to work and they told me he had died. Passed away in his sleep. Probably next to that Johnny Walker bottle. . . . I'm going to miss that old boy. Miss his habit and miss his stories. But most of all I'm going to miss those nice tips. *(Reflects for a moment)* Yeah, I'm going to miss them real bad.

Holding up his drink and offers a toast.

To you, Monsignor, wherever you are.

An Old, Old Story

Ruth, a woman in her early forties

Now this story is an old one, but it needs to be told and retold till everybody get the point and this whole business stops. *(Pause)* When I first heard it, I was only eight or nine. My great, great, great must've told it to my great, great, and my great, great told it to my Gran who told it to my mother who then told it to me.

It's about this pretty, pretty girl who was born into a slave family. From the time she was six everybody could tell she was going to be a beauty, including the master. So right from the beginning, he had her marked for special food, special clothes, special favors, and a special arrangement up in his bedroom when the child hit thirteen. Now it didn't seem to matter much to this man that he had a wife and two daughters older than this pretty black girl. And wasn't anybody who could say much to him because this man was very much the master of his house. So, whenever he was in the mood that child had to spend the night on his bed. And whenever she come down in the morning, that child was always in pain and asking her mama what she could do not to have to spend another night up in that man's room.

Her mother told her, "Pray." So the child did. Three times a day she got on her knees and said her prayers to the Lord.

Now it just so happened that the mother was the cook for this house and she know how to make some special dishes that the master loved a whole lot.

It also just happened that there was a bush down the road that all the slaves knew was poison. All you had to do was put one leaf of it in somebody's food and it was "Goodbye to this world, hello to the next."

Well, the mama didn't do it all at once, but a little at a time. She'd cut the leaf up real fine and mix it in his soup. Or put it in with his collard greens and spinach. It took the man about seven months to die, and the doctors couldn't figure out why. He just got sicker and sicker until one day he wasn't here anymore. The girl said, "Mama, the Lord answered my prayer." And the mama said, "Yes. The power of prayers should never be underestimated."

Well, that story took place again recently with a woman I know. Only this time the color scheme changed. Everybody involved was black. And the man wasn't a master but the husband of the woman and the father of the child he was taking advantage of.

Now the mother could've gone to the police and filled out a report. Then there would've been an investigation, a trial, maybe a mistrial, publicity, TV news stories, and all kinds of ugly talk while the wheels of justice take its careful time to make up its mind.

Well, she couldn't wait that long and neither could her used-to-be innocent, thirteen-year-old daughter. And it just so happened that the mother knew a little bit about chemicals and poisons just from reading all those mystery novels she likes to pass the time of day with. And she also knew something about cooking his favorite foods. This was a man the woman used to be in love with. So much so that she married him and had this child in good faith. But something went wrong and now she couldn't stand the sight of him, based on what he was doing to their daughter.

The first sign was when he start complaining about cramps in his stomach. She told him to go to the hospital but he wasn't a man who liked anything to do with doctors or hospitals. So all he did was take aspirin after aspirin after aspirin after aspirin. By the time the doctors got there, it was too late. They said taking all them aspirins burned a hole in his stomach as big as a quarter. Wasn't nothing they could do. The cause of death was attributed to "natural causes." She gave him a nice funeral and even pretended to cry. Her daughter is fine and seems to be forgetting the whole thing. Now there's only one person left that should start doing some forgetting and that person is: the woman herself. Bartender, another one please. It seem like a minute ago this glass was full, now it's empty. So fill me up again, please.

A Puzzlement

Ronny, early thirties

Ask me about love and I'll talk about sex. Ask me about sex and I'll talk about memories. It all gets mixed up sometimes. The real, the unreal. The fantasy and the facts. But who cares anymore. It's all the same in the final analysis. Isn't it? . . . Of course it is. Why would it not be? *(Pause)*

I picked up this guy in a bar. I won't tell you where or when. Or even who I was at the time. Enough to say he was there, I was there, and something drew us together. He asked if I wanted to dance and I said, "Sure." . . . So we danced. . . .

Music creeps into the background as the memory takes hold.

He looked into my eyes and told me I was attractive. I told him he was, too. Although it wasn't strictly true. But what do you say when someone pays you a compliment. You give it back in kind. He wasn't ugly like a beast or anything. He just wasn't handsome in the way most people measure those things. But what are looks anyway? Just a covering that hides the good or the rot that's inside. Isn't that so? . . . Anyway, we danced and kissed and then we danced some more. He said he had come to the club with a friend but that it was okay. So we kissed and danced some more. Later we left and walked from one side of town to the other touching and talking. Then he stopped and said, "This is where I live. Want to come up?"

"What about your roommate?" I asked. "He has his room, I have mine," he told me, cupping his hand and squeezing me gently. "And he won't bother us. Not unless you want him to." With that he smiled a really charming smile. But I told him no. "One is enough for me. And you'll do just fine." Again he smiled that charming smile and we were inside his place and into his bedroom in what seemed like a matter of minutes.

He was gentle and rough and then gentle again. And so was I. Or maybe I'm not remembering although it only happened yesterday or the day before. Or was it actually longer than that? *(Pause while he tries to remember, then decides not to bother)* Anyway, who cares? It happened and now it's past, and now it's here, and that's the facts.

Now I wasn't dreaming. No, I wasn't dreaming but it felt like I was. Because somewhere, somewhere in the middle of the night, or in the middle of our night, as it were, I realized that there wasn't just one body in the bed with me, but two. Him and the phantom roommate. That's right, him and the other person I'd never met. Now in this era of plague that we're all living through, you worry about all sorts of things. But sometimes, just sometimes you find yourself saying, "The hell with it. Just go with the flow." And that's what I did. I went with the flow. The river took me upstream, then downstream, then upstream and down again. After which I surrendered to the god of sleep and let him take me into that other world.

Morning came, I sat up and looked around. I was alone in the bed. I could hear them in the kitchen talking and laughing. The radio or TV was playing and I could even smell coffee brewing. The bathroom was next door so I went in, showered, got dressed, and combed my hair. When I got to the kitchen I said, "Good morning." The conversation stopped. Nobody spoke. . . . The roommate was reading the newspaper, so I asked, "What's the headline?" Again I got no answer. Not even a stare. "What's the matter?" I said, trying to get their attention. The room-mate just threw the paper on the table, got up, and went back to his room. My friend just sat there sipping his coffee, looking off in a direction as though deep in thought. "What's the matter with him?" I asked. "I thought we had a good time last night. What's the matter with you? I'm just trying to say hello." He didn't answer again but he moved. He got up and went to the window and just stood there in his bathrobe, looking out.

"Did I do something wrong? What the hell's the matter? What's going on? Talk to me, damn you! Talk to me." Finally when I could take it no longer I went over and grabbed at his shoulder. "Don't treat me like this. Say something to me please. Tell me what's going on. Talk to me or else." And with that I guess I shook him. Shook him kinda hard. And the next thing I knew all the wind was rushing out of me. Rushing out of me fast. He had punched me hard in the stomach and I was finding it impossible to breathe. So I just stood there frozen and gasping for breath. The last time I remember being hit that hard was when I was a kid. I had smart mouthed an older boy and he didn't like it. So without saying anything he turned and slammed me in the gut. And I remember, too, gasping for breath and not being able to get it.

I guess I must've fallen to the floor but I don't remember it. All I remember is lying there with the furniture and walls moving back and forth before me. And black spots circling just in front of my eyes.

Finally I managed to get myself up. There was nobody in the kitchen. Just me and the coffee in the machine and the paper still lying there on the table. The TV or radio I'd heard before was off now. Everything was silence. I made it to the door, down the elevator and out to the sidewalk where I caught a cab and went home. The next three hours were spent in the bathtub trying to soothe the pain in my gut and wondering what the hell that was all about. And you want to know something? I still haven't figured it out.

Something Artistic

Tiny, late twenties, the waitress

I wish I could dance, sing, play music, or do something more artistic than standing here serving drinks. When I was in school I used to draw. People said I had talent but nothing ever come of it. No. There was too many other things I had to do at the time.

Had me a boyfriend but he joined the Army and never came back. Wrote me a few letters saying how much he love me. Then he stopped writing and that was that. . . . Got me another one but he wound up in jail for trying to be slick. When he got out he was a different person. The Muslims had got to him. Said I had to change my way of life and change my beliefs if I still wanted to be with him. I couldn't do that so he was gone, too. Then like a fool I up and got married. He's gone, too. I don't know where. He's out there somewhere but only God in heaven know where that is. Lucky for us we didn't have no children, not that we didn't work at it. We did. Got pregnant twice but each time something went wrong. And each time I had a miscarriage. I don't know why, but that's the way things turned out. I think he blamed me for the miscarriages. He didn't exactly say so, but I think that's what he did. And I also think that's why he left without saying a word.

Well, that's how it goes sometimes, doesn't it. "No use in crying over spilled milk," my mother used to say, God rest her soul. No. No use in crying at all. Still, I woulda liked to have them babies. Woulda liked to have them both. But it wasn't meant to be. Nooo, it wasn't meant to be at all.

I should've kept up with my artwork, come to think it. I was good. I was damn good. But it's too late now. Just too damn late. You see, talent is like a plant. You got to feed and water it if you want it to grow. And you got to nourish it, too. If you don't, it dies. It just withers up and dies. And that's what happened to mine. It just withered up and died . . . Poof.

Taking It Slow

Mr. Aubrey, a man in his late sixties

Young boys today don't know how to be with a woman and that's a fact. They don't know nothing about being romantic and being soft. All they seem to know about is how to throw her down, pull her clothes off, and jump on her. Then when they satisfied, get up, put on their clothes, and go. No buildup, no suspense, no seduction. Just bam, bam, bam, and go. The amazing thing to me is that the women let them get away with it.

In my day you had to sweet-talk a woman. Beg, plead, promise all kinds of things, and sometimes you even had to say a prayer or two. Then if you was lucky she might feel sorry for you and let you get a little. . . . Sound hard? Was hard. But I'll tell you something, when you got there it was worth all the effort. And you was appreciative. Damn appreciative.

Nowadays, you try to sweet-talk a girl and she look at you like you a fool. Or maybe you crazy. They ain't interested in none a that. They want what the young boys want. Some quick and easy action with no complication. But you see, to me that's a shame because the complication is where the fun was. Now it's just dry. Quick and dry. Kinda like shaking hands or something.

People tell me I'm old. Want to know the truth? I'm glad I am. Glad I grew up in the time I did. You all move too fast. Do things too quick. I like it nice and slow. Nice and easy and relaxed. That's how I eat, that's how I drink, that's how I do everything these days. Even when I was young I was that way. And ain't ever found any reason to change. No sir, no reason at all.

(Calling to off stage) Bobby! Bobby! Give everybody a drink. On me. Tell them it's from the old man. Tell them to drink it slow. Savor the taste and the flavor. And Bobby, give me another one so I can do the same.

Dreams: A Warning

Ben, late twenties

Tell you about dreams, man. Dreams is the best and worst things that ever was. Dreams is what used to make it possible for me to look out of the window of my dingy room. Thinking about places I'd never been and faces I never knew that lived somewhere past all them dirty-looking buildings and that aluminum-colored sky.

I wasn't working so there was a lot of time for looking. A lot of time for dreaming.

People would talk, car horns would blow, and the TV would make its noise from morning till night. But none of that ever interrupt my thoughts. None of it could interrupt my dreaming.

Time passed. Days into months. Months into years. And if you had put a statue in that window looking out at all them rooftops, that statue could've been me. Just sitting there, thinking hard . . . dreaming.

Dreaming about what? Clothes, cars, women, food, beaches, nightclubs, and music. All kinds of music.

Music that could fill your soul and take you away from dirty rooms and lonely nights. Music that could take you away from stupid jobs and empty pockets. Away from friends who weren't friends. And women who smile at you but won't give you anything more than that smile.

"Tomorrow will be better," the dreams tell you. "Tomorrow will be great. Just wait and see."

Everyday you wake up and tomorrow is where all the golden dreams is. Tomorrow is when it'll all come true.

Then one day it comes to you. The dream was the reality and the reality was the dream. . . . Or is it the other way around? . . . That's what I mean. You get confused. And you're not sure if you coming or you going. That's the time to stop. 'Cause if you don't, those dreams will eat you. They'll eat your whole life and you'll wonder where it went. That's what I mean when I say dreams is both good and bad. Dreams can be a lover, but they can be a monster, too. So watch out for them, okay?

Best Excuse in the World

Eugenie, mid thirties

I don't know why I got involved. Love, I suppose. Isn't that the best excuse in the world for all the dumb things we do in our lives? You just say: "I was in love," and everybody understands. Love . . . love . . . love . . . love.

I didn't think it was possible to love somebody the way I loved Billy. When I was with him I felt like a child again. A little child with her daddy, all warm and cuddly. He used to call me his "Baby." His "teeny, weenie baby," and big as I am I used to feel tiny and safe. I would've done anything for that man. Anything at all. But he didn't ask for anything. All he said he ever wanted was to have me near so he could hold me forever. Just to hold me forever. Isn't that nice? . . .

When I was a girl my father always used to warn me not to trust happiness. Pop was a drunk and a loser but he always used to say: "Baby, whatever you do, don't ever trust in happiness. If you do it'll betray you every time. Every time." Pop was a character. *(Pause)*

Billy said he loved me and wanted to spend the rest of his life with me. We made plans for our wedding every time we were together. I was dancing at the time and making good money. When we went to meet his mother, I tried to look my best and act even better. . . . But I could tell from the moment that woman took a look at me, it was hate at first sight. But she didn't show it any obvious ways. She did just the opposite. She smiled, then gave me a hug and a kiss. But I could tell that woman couldn't stand me. That woman couldn't even stand the space I was taking up or the air I was breathing. No sir, that woman didn't like me at all. When I mentioned it to Billy later that night, he said I was just imagining things. Said his mother was a wonderful woman who liked anyone he loved. But, three months later when he told me we were finished, I know I wasn't imagining things then.

"It was your mother, wasn't it?" I asked. "She didn't think I was classy enough or social enough for her little black boy, did she?"

He didn't answer, but we both knew I was telling the truth. Every time we'd get together all that woman could talk about was what good schools Billy went to, and what fine professionals all the other members of his family were. And I had nothing to match that. Just working-class people who either went to church or to bars.

Billy left and I started to drift from one man to another. Searching for another Billy, I suppose. Another man to make me feel cuddly and warm. Of course that was a waste of time but I couldn't help myself. I even got married once. That was a big mistake as I think I ever made. I won't do that again anytime soon. No sir.

So—here I am, the same place my father ended up. In a bar, with a drink at ten o'clock in the morning. Pop was onto something. I didn't know it then, but I sure as hell know it now.

Man in the News

Olivia, late thirties

Scary people are just that. Scary. They're not like you and me. They live by other standards and different rules. And the only thing you and I can do is stay away from them. Far, far away.

I had a drink with him once because I knew his brother, Joshua. We went out together for a while. And for a period of about a year it looked like we might even get married. So he would've been family if we had hitched. But as it turned out, we didn't.

Joshua had told me about his younger brother, Omar. How smart Omar was, how good looking, and how he went and messed himself up with the law.

It seems that when Omar was nineteen him and another guy decided to rob this old man late one night. But when they jumped him, the old man put up a fight. In the struggle, the old man fell and hit his head on the sidewalk, cracking open his skull. He was dead before the paramedics got there. The two guys took off before the police arrived. But someone had seen them and they were arrested a few hours later. Bail was set and his father put up his house as collateral. The feeling was that because of his youth, Omar would get minimum time. Three, four, no more than five years max.

Omar agreed and everything looked fine. Then one morning when the family woke up he was gone. He had decided not to wait around for some judge to pronounce sentence. Their father lost his home and died two years later in a fire at a transient hotel.

Years went by and one day he contacted Joshua to ask if

he could visit. Josh said yes because Omar was the only family he had and he didn't want to lose him. Omar was a full-time criminal now, Joshua told me. His specialty was robbing banks in small towns. They'd go in, grab the cash, and get out quick. The money wasn't much but it was enough to keep him happy. Then something went wrong. There was a shoot-out and two bank people were killed. Omar was on the run from the Feds and he needed a place to lay low for a few days.

"Why are you doing this?" I asked. "Why are you letting him stay at your place?"

"Because he's my brother and I got to help him," Josh said. "Bad as he is, I don't want to see him hurt or in jail. It's as simple as that."

I met Omar during that visit. He was everything Joshua had said. Good-looking, alert, and with a bright friendly smile. You would never guess he was a man on the run. There was nothing nervous or shifty about him. . . . Something I didn't tell Joshua is that Omar tried to score on me. It happened when Josh went to the bathroom. Omar, without preamble, leaned over and said to me, "You're an interesting woman. We should talk together, you and me. Late at night sometime when there ain't no other ears to hear us."

"I don't think so," I told him.

"Shame," he said. "Could've been something for your memory book."

It was a little over a year later when Josh got a call from a friend that Omar had been picked up and was in jail. The charge was murder. Omar and two others were in the process of robbing a bar one night after the place was closed, when the manager, who they knew, walked in on them. They tied him up, put a gag in his mouth, and finished what they were doing. As they were about to leave, Omar said they had to do something about the manager. The man could identify them. One guy suggested they leave the state, but Omar had a better idea. He turned the man around and stabbed him in the back several times. "Dead men can't talk to nobody." The others were shocked but didn't say anything. They just got out of the place fast.

A month later the cops knocked on the door and he was arrested for a murder everyone thought would go unsolved. He had been named by one of the guys he was with who had gotten religion and said that he couldn't sleep due to the vicious act they committed that night.

Omar was sentenced to die by lethal injection. People wrote letters, met with the lawyers, talked to politicians, and tried everything they could. It dragged on for several years. In that time Josh and I broke up. He went his way and I went mine.

It's over now. The last appeal ran out. So Omar was taken to a room, strapped to a table, and in the presence of witnesses they put the poison in him.

I saw the item in the paper this morning over coffee and for some reason I feel depressed. I don't know why. I just do. If I hadn't met him he would just be another name in the paper. But I did and for some reason, I can't get him out of my mind.

THE PROJECTS

The projects of the big cities is where so many of us live out our lives. Detroit, Philly, Brooklyn, LA, Cleveland, Newark, and New York. . . . We live here, we die here, and in between we reach for a memory, reach for a dream.

Or sometimes we just stand still and wait . . . for the future to happen.

Moving Around

Tony P., late twenties

That was so damn funny. I still don't believe it. Sometimes, sometimes you get the feeling that the Lord looking out for you special. But the truth is, it might even be the devil. . . . I was staying in an apartment just down the street, and the woman I was messing with was giving me all kinds of trouble. See—she had this stepdaughter name Stephanie, visiting for a week. And Stephanie and I got to making the moon smile, if you know what I mean.

Now I ain't no fool and don't want to kill the goose by doing anything obvious. But I also know that opportunity knock only once. So that night when Alice went out and Stephanie start up playing her games, I figure, "Hey—why the hell not? God give you a chance, you better shoot or pass the dice." 'Sides, our secret would be safe. What could she do? Tell Alice she was messing up the bed with the old lady's man? Hell no, no woman ain't that dumb, especially no girl in heat like Stephanie was. And she was in heat, let me tell you. She was like a machine gun ready to go off. And I damn sure wasn't going to say nothing. So everything was cool, right? . . . Wrong. Goddamn wrong. Stephanie must've said something. Because the next day and the days after that Alice start acting quiet and strange. She didn't say anything while Steph was around, but I could tell by her attitude things wasn't like they used to be.

After Stephanie left she told me that I should start looking for a place. That things wasn't working out and her neighbors in the building was beginning to talk. Before she didn't give a damn 'bout the neighbors, now she was getting concerned all over the place. Hey—I ain't never been one for no scenes with no woman. 'Specially when I'm a guest in that woman's house. You give them trouble or go upside their head and they start calling cop. And you and I know black cop like nothing better than to put some knots in your head with their billy club whenever some woman is involved. So I didn't argue. I didn't say nothing. I took the lady's suggestion and start hitting the pavement. . . . I coulda used a little more time, but I could see the woman wanted me out in a hurry. So one night while she was asleep I grabbed my little bit of stuff, took all the money she had in her purse, and got me a hotel room. It was nice not having to wake up just because she had to and nice not having to get into any kinda bedroom action when I wasn't in the mood. So, all in all, things wasn't so bad. No they wasn't bad at all. . . . I was in that hotel room a whole damn week when I run into Tricia on the sidewalk that morning and she was looking okay. Not great, but not bad either. She had put on some weight. I could see that. I could see that right away. Some people might even call her fat. But hell, I ain't never been against no woman putting on an extra pound here and there. Just gives me more to hold on to, know what I mean? *(He laughs)* Anyway, she greet me like I was some long lost relative. Gave me her number and said we had to get together. Now that was kind of a surprise after the way we broke up five years ago. I mean we didn't have no fight or nothing like that. I just took off after she told me that stuff about being pregnant and all. Took off like a jackrabbit and didn't look back. Last person I expected to run into was her. Now here she was hugging me and offering to make me dinner sometime. So I said okay and went over to her place.

Well, to make a long story short, I'm living in these

projects again. I think this place is my destiny. Tricia is the fifth woman I been shacked up with in here. It would be kinda boring if it wasn't for the fact that I ain't paying no rent. And you know what they say: Beggars can't be choosers. And what the hell, a project is a project is a project is a project. Ain't that so?

Coming to Terms

Maya, late twenties

Oh God, oh God, you're not going to make me sorry I told you about my life before we met, are you?

Something told me I shouldn't'a said anything, shoulda kept it all inside and let it be. But I didn't want to do that. I didn't want any secrets between us. I wanted you to know all about me, just like I want to know all about you. So I told you 'bout the guys. All of them. And all the things we done, too. I also told you how things were and what I was going through at the time. . . . Look, look, I told you all that stuff because I wanted you to know who I was. And how I got to where you found me. Where we found each other. You understand? I hope you do. I want you to. I'm a person. That's all, just a person. Not a saint, not a sinner, just a person. I'm not that old but I had a life, a sex life before I met you. I did a lot of things. Things I'm not proud of. It was crap, it was garbage, but I did them and now it's gone. What do you want me to do, go back in time and undo them? I can't, you can't, nobody can. So we have to live with it, that's all.

Look, I married you because I love you. Out of the mess and confusion of life in this city we bumped into each other and found something special. Something worth committing our whole lives to. And I'm willing and I'm trying, but it's not going to work if we start dredging up the past. A past you only know about because I told you.

You want to live in Disneyland and pretend that I was a virgin before you met me, that's your problem. For me, I want to live in the real world. And if that's too much for you, then you better tell me now.

Forty Deuce Street

Ike, mid forties

You looking at me and I'm going to tell you the truth. You looking at a worried man. I'm worried because I'm looking at 42d Street and I see a form and a way of life just getting blown away by dynamite and drills, construction workers and cement, Disneyland and Mickey Mouse. I look at it and it make me cry. Cry in my heart because I remember how it was. How it used to be. Now don't get me wrong. The place wasn't perfect. Hell no, that place wasn't perfect at all. But it wasn't plastic either. That place had life, and that's what I'm going to miss. The life.

One night I was in this movie theatre and this woman just started screaming and screaming. People kept yelling for her to "shut up!" But she just kept on screaming and screaming. Finally they stopped the movie and turned on the lights. Know what we saw? The man sitting next to the woman had his head down and his chest all covered with blood. Somebody had cut his throat from one side to the next.

Another night I was waiting in line trying to see this film but the woman in the ticket booth was on the phone talking with somebody and holding the whole line up. So the cat in front of me said, "Sister, you got to do one a two things. Either you got to put down that phone and sell us some tickets, or close the booth and tell us all to go to hell."

The woman in the booth told her friend on the phone, "Excuse me." And look up at the cat and said, "Why don't you kiss my behind and mind your own business?" At the same time she take the brother's five dollars, punched up a ticket, and gave him change as though he had given her a twenty. I was behind so she sold me a ticket and I followed him into the lobby. Now I couldn't resist saying something, so I said: "Serve her right, nasty hussy."

"What you talking 'bout?" he said, eyes darting around like he was scared.

"I saw what happened. And I'm saying it serve her right that she give you change for a twenty when you only gave her a five."

"Oh, you see that, eh?"

"Yeah."

Then he start to relax. "Well, you see, that's what happens when you in the state of Grace. God take care of you. See, only one man would make a piece of good luck like that happen. That's our Father in the Sky. Are you in the state of Grace, my man?"

Oh God, my mind begin to groan. Not another one of these. I was instantly sorry I said anything to the man. He wanted to share the money with me and talk about God. Finally, I had to leave the theatre to get away from him.

Damn, I been going to them movie theatres for years, and I can't think of a time I just walk in and watch the movie when something in there didn't happen. If it wasn't two brothers having it out, it was some other commotion going on that would draw everybody's attention away from the flick. Like the night we was all sitting there watching this karate thing with a lot of Chinese folks running around kicking each other. This brother called out to the cat sitting in front of him. "Hey, bro, you got to sit down low in that seat or something. Your head is too big and I can't see the screen." Now that kind of stuff is unreasonable. How can you blame a man for his head being too big? But this cat did and he wouldn't let up on my man. He kept kicking the seat and talking out till the cat with the big head said, "Man, why don't you leave me alone? I ain't bothering you, all I'm trying to do is watch this damn movie." But the cat, who had to be a bully, just wouldn't let up on my man. Somebody even called out: "Hey baby if you can't see why don't you move?"

"Hell no, I ain't going nowhere. I ain't the one with the big goddamn head. He is. A cat with a head that size shouldn't be allowed in the theatre in the first place." With that he kick the seat some more while the folks around them laughed. Now I got to confess, I did a little laughing myself. Anyway the man with the big head who wasn't a big man, matter of fact he was kind a small, got up and said, "Alright, brother man, I hope you happy, I'm going to move."

(Doing two voices) "Damn right you going to move. You didn't have no other choice."

"Now all the people here are my witnesses. I didn't bother you, you bother me."

"So what? You planning to call a cop or something?"

"No. I'm just going to go," the big-headed brother said in a quiet voice, "but when I come back, I hope you still here."

"Why?"

"No reason. I just hope so that's all." And with that my man left.

Well, there was a little murmuring in the crowd and people start to move away from the cat with the big mouth.

"Hey, what's going on?"

"I heard what the man said and I don't want to be here. Cat sound like he coming back with a gun."

"That fool?"

"May be a fool. Maybe not. May be a man with a weapon stashed someplace. Anyhow I don't want to take no chances. Cat could be bluffing. But on the other side bullets ain't got no eye. I might get hit by one of the strays."

Well, like I said, the area got clear. Finally, the only one left was Mister Big Mouth saying, "I ain't scared. I got me a weapon, too." But he was trying to save face and we all knew it. Then somebody said, "I think I see the cat coming back. Ain't that the big head Brother that was just here?" Now wasn't anybody of the kind, but my man head snap around. After a while every new person that walk into the theatre people was saying was our man coming back. Finally, even Mister Big Mouth had to get up and go, 'cause he wasn't sure. And he wasn't enjoying the flick. Matter of fact, he wasn't even seeing it since he was turning around so much. You see, that man in his quiet way fixed that fool but good. All he said was one sentence, but it put so much worry in his mind the fool had to split. That's how you can fix a man without touching him. Tell you something else. The cat with the big head didn't leave the theatre. He was sitting in the balcony all the time that other stuff was going on.

42d Street, boy, that place was a trip. . . . Now it all gone. The city taking down them buildings and putting up hotels and stuff. Say it gon' make the city nicer and safer. Maybe. But I'll tell you the truth, I'm going to miss the way it used to be. I'm going to miss all the fun and the action. *(Looking around)* This is what they call "progress" I suppose. Out with the old, on with the new. . . . Still I'm going to miss it. It breaks my heart to see it go. Yes, it sure does.

Quietly he exits.

Six Weeks

Venessa, nineteen years old

I can't say nothing, of course. So I just have to walk around pretending I'm dumb and that I don't know who the father of my child is. All I can say is that there were so many boys I was messing with that I don't know which one got me pregnant. Of course it ain't true. Of course it's a damn lie. And of course I know who the father is. What am I, a fool? But that's my story and I'm sticking to it. Because if I tell the truth things gon' be even worst than they are already.

I mean right now I'm pregnant and Mama's pregnant and we both schedule to have the baby within six weeks of each other. Six weeks, can you believe that? Mama say she gon' help me through mine if I help her through hers. Of course, I will and soon this place gon' be full of crying babies. Aunt Florence say she don't understand none of it. Now she helping us through it, too. But she say it out plain. She just don't understand how the two of us could go out and get pregnant at the same time. And what I know she find hard to believe is the fact that I don't know who the father of my baby is. See, I ain't never been a girl known to run around with a lot of boys. Now all of a sudden I'm pregnant and I'm saying there was so many that I don't know who.

"Something wrong with that explanation," Aunt Florence say, "something ain't right about it at all." But my mother told her to leave me alone. "The girl got enough problems, let's not go pushing her to tell us something she don't know, or maybe don't want to tell." So Aunt Florence backed off, but I know she ain't convinced. I can see it every time she look at me.

The man that got my Mama pregnant is JP. They been seeing each other for nearly four years now. JP got a wife in Brooklyn that he say he planning on divorcing. But I don't believe none of it. JP been telling that story ever since he met my mama and nothing ain't change. I don't think Mama believe it either. But she just keep hoping things will change. You see, since my daddy died, she been out with a few men but none of them turn out to be much. JP is the best, far and away. He even give her money to help run the house and stuff. I don't know how much his wife know about this, but JP spend a lot of his time here with us in the projects. Sometimes three weekends a month. I know he also got two kids. Boys. What they're doing during that time, I have no idea. But when he's here, he takes Mama and me out to the movies and stuff. Fixes things around the place and even helped me with my schoolwork sometimes. It's kinda like he's the man a two houses. And I like him. I like him a lot. I like him because as strong as he is, I mean taking care of two homes, a man got to be strong, he's weak. The reason I know it is because he told me so. One night when Mama called and said she had to work a double shift because somebody didn't show up, JP came over and we got to watching TV and talking. Next thing we was kissing and touching on each other in all kinds a ways. Now this wasn't such a surprise because him and me had been eyeing each other for a while now but not saying anything about it. Suddenly this night it all come out in a rush.

Afterwards he cried and told me he was weak, and that he couldn't help himself. He asked me to forgive him. I told him there was nothing to forgive because I loved him. And I do. I still do. So we continued whenever we got the chance. Sometimes here, sometimes someplace else.

"I want to end it with your mother," he told me. "But

I want to do it gently. I don't want to hurt her." And the truth is, I don't want to hurt her either.

That's what we were working toward when Mama came home and announced that she was pregnant. Mama is forty and this may be one of her last chances at having a baby, so she's in heaven over this.

Three weeks later I had the same announcement to make. JP talk to me about getting an abortion, but I told him no. This baby is the proof of the love that we got between us and I ain't giving that up. No, I ain't giving that up at all. But I can't say nothing to Mama about who the father is, because it would kill her. It would just kill her.

So Mama is here, JP is here, and I am here. In six weeks there gon' be two new additions to our family, and one man who is the father to them both.

Remembering Teddy

Clarence, early forties

Ever had the situation where you sitting around thinking about one thing and for some reason or another a name pops into your head? And all of a sudden you're off in a whole other direction thinking about a whole other thing? This happened to me today with Teddy. We weren't exactly friends or anything like that. We were coworkers at this hotshot restaurant on the East Side. I had been there for a while and was considered the best waiter in the place. Then Teddy came in (three years after me) and about two weeks into his being there it was hinted at by the powers in the place that not only was he as good a waiter as I was, but perhaps better. Maybe even sensational. They talked about his speed, his efficiency, his know-how. All this was meant to rankle I knew. I had been there a while and perhaps they felt I was getting a little superior or smug about my position. I guess I should also add that Teddy was white and I was black. Not that it had much to do with the situation. But it's always a factor even when that factor is subliminal. So make of it what you like. The point being that I was prepared to dislike Teddy but found that once we worked together a few times I didn't dislike him at all. In fact, it was just the opposite. I liked him. I liked him a lot. And I saw what they meant about his waiting skills. He was terrific. He told me that he had been trained by one of the top hotel and restaurant schools in the country and had been an executive for a large restaurant chain until his drinking problem cost him his job. Now he was trying to work his way back via waiting tables in restaurants such as this one. I asked about his drinking problem and he said it was "reduced." But I noticed that he kept a little flask of vodka behind the waiters' station, which he mixed with water and sipped from all day. It never made him drunk. It just kept him upbeat, I think.

Now, Teddy was so good that they took him off waiting tables for two days a week and told him he had to seat people. Teddy protested because as a waiter he was making more than twice as much as the salary they were paying for him to seat people. But they told him he had no choice. The other three days he worked with me, he complained, because in practical terms, this advancement he had gotten resulted in a cut in his pay. Then, to make things worse, within a few weeks he was taken off waiting tables completely and made a full-time maitre d'. I told him, "Congratulations." He scowled at me and said, "I hate it. I really, really hate it. What they're doing to me isn't fair. It just isn't fair." But he continued doing it for months on end. Never complaining to them, only to me. *(Brief pause)*

One afternoon I walked into work and saw that the place was in turmoil. We were supposed to be getting ready to open but the owners and managers were standing around in clusters frowning and talking and pointing at things. Before I could ask what was going on the manager walked up to me and asked how well I knew Teddy.

"Not well," I said. "In fact, I hardly knew him at all. We just worked together, that's all. Why?"

I was then told that Teddy had stolen over thirty thousand dollars from the restaurant the night before. You see, part of his job as maitre d' was to put the restaurant's receipts in the night deposit drop at the end of his shift. Apparently that night he didn't and when they went looking for him, he was gone. He lived in a transient hotel. The desk clerk said he had paid his bill and left. To where? The desk clerk had no idea.

Everyone was upset. "Teddy. Imagine that. Quiet, decent Teddy doing a thing like that? I wonder what happened to him?"

I wasn't surprised. I hadn't seen it coming but I still wasn't surprised. I was pleased. In a secret way, I was happy for Teddy and wished him well. Ever since he had put on that tuxedo and began seating people, Teddy looked like a man trapped in a cell. The money he stole I hoped would liberate him, I was sure. I envied him. Because I felt trapped in this job, too. I needed to make some renegade move to free myself. But I didn't have the guts or imagination or whatever. I simply didn't have it and I hated myself for that.

"Bravo Teddy! Bravo." . . . Of course I didn't say that out loud. But I thought it. Oh boy did I think it.

Unfortunately, his run didn't last long. They tracked him down in San Francisco but couldn't prove conclusively that he had stolen the money. So he got off scot-free. He even sent me a card once saying, "I know you think about me and worry about me. Don't. I'm fine. Teddy."

A year and a half later he was found dead in his room. A victim of internal bleeding. When asked about personal possessions he had only a few items. Among them was a bank book with a balance of eight thousand dollars. He was a good waiter all right. The best I ever worked with. That's for damn sure.

What It's All About

Floyd, eighteen years old

I know nobody want to hear this but I'm gonna say it any-how, just to get it said.

I had me a cousin name Wilbert and he had a sister name Vinette. Now this sister had a different mother, so we wasn't related at all. Wilbert had light skin and straight hair—and for some reason, everybody liked him. Said he had a nice personality and was smart. . . . One day we was just sitting around talking about things when he told me that his sister like to do it with boys. Said she was doing it with him all the time but now she wanted to do it with somebody else, too. So I said yes and we started doing it in threes. Wilbert first and me next. We used to meet once or twice a week when her aunt was out at work. I would stand guard as a lookout while Wilbert was getting it on and he would then turn around and stand guard for me.

Don't you know that one day the aunt came in and caught me in the act. Where Wilbert was, I don't know. All I know is my pants was down and his aunt was standing over me and Vinette shouting, "Oh my God! Oh my God!" Then she started hitting me and screaming for the police. Vinette musta said something about rape because the next thing I know, I was in handcuffs and people was saying that I was some kind a animal. That I wasn't fit to live among civilized folks.

In juvenile court the aunt said she heard a scream and when she came in she saw Vinette resisting and me forcing her down. When it was time for Vinette to testify, all she said was, "I'd rather not talk about it anymore if you don't mind." And that's when the DA said, "Your Honor, are we going to put this poor child through this ordeal again?" And of course they didn't. My lawyer said it was better for me if she didn't testify. He said my best chance was a plea bargain. That's what he did. And got me eighteen months. The truth is, they had me guilty the moment I was accused and there was nothing I could say that would change anybody's mind. They were going through the motions. Everybody, including my lawyer. So I let it happen. I stood there and listened. And when I was asked what I had to say for myself, I said: "Nothing, your Honor."

"You sure?"

"Yes, sir."

That's when he said, "Well, you leave this court no other choice than to sentence you to eighteen months in juvenile prison where it is hoped that you will reflect on what you have done, acquire some sense of remorse, and resolve to change your life for the better."

"Eighteen months!" some people called out. "Animal like that should get ten years or life in adult prison! Bastard like that got to be kept off the streets and away from decent people."

And my mother, what did she do? She just looked at me. Looked at me and cried. I was a real bastard now. First being born without a father. And now being accused of this terrible thing.

Some months into my time Wilbert came to see me. All he could say was, "I'm sorry man. I'm really, really sorry." . . . I told him to hell with it. That's the way the dice roll sometimes. He asked how I was getting on, I told him "Okay." He came by a few more times to bring me cigarettes and stuff. Then he disappeared. But on his last trip I asked him how was Vinette. He told me she had run off with some cab-driving dude and that her aunt was all upset. I laughed and Wilbert laughed, too. "I guess they can't say rape this time."

"No, I guess not." After that I didn't see Wilbert again.

It was three days after my eighteenth birthday when they let me out. The truth is, I didn't mind being inside. It was a lot more interesting than high school. And the people were a lot more straight. Most of the time. That don't mean it was easy. But I could handle it. It was all about survival and that was just fine with me.

I'm out now and I'm ready. I can live in this world of yours because now I know what you're all about.

A Military Man

Jake, mid forties, is dressed in old military garb

Listen here and listen up good! I picked up a woman with four children and a dead husband. And all their lives I support them, loved them, and tried to bring them up to be functioning boys and girls. That's right. That's what I did. Now let me ask you a question. What man in his right mind would do something like that? Huh? What man? Most men I knew was trying to get out of responsibilities, not deeper into them. And now what's my reward? What's my thank-you for all this? It's eleven o'clock at night and my wife is across the street rolling around on a bed with some damn musician just because he's fifteen years younger and plays on some stupid jazz CD that nobody want to buy.

Hell, everybody in this house think I'm a fool. That I don't know what's going on. They think that because a person don't say much, he don't see what's happening around him. But I got eyes and I got ears. This neighborhood ain't that big. People talk and I hear. And I know. Believe me, when I tell you I know. But I'm watching them. I am goddamned watching them. That's what they trained me for with twenty years in the U.S. military. To develop my instincts and sniff out the enemy. I can sniff out danger like a jungle animal. I have the instincts of a cheetah. That's right, a goddamn cheetah.

You don't know who I am. But I'll tell you who I am. I am an ex-U.S. Army official with a sergeant's stripes and a pension to prove it. I'm a man who's been in combat and knows what the smell of battle is like.

Fort Knox, Kentucky, where they keep all the gold, is where they saw fit to have a man like me serve. I used to guard this nation's treasure. When I walked through those barracks on inspection day, grown men used to shake in their drawers. That's right, shake in their drawers! Black, white, green, it didn't matter. They used to shake! I was a man with power. Military power. They don't know who they messing with. . . . No sir! They don't have the slightest idea. Not a notion. Not a clue. But they'll find out one day. You wait. They are going to find out good!

It Just Goes to Show

Clemmie, mid forties

No matter how you look on it, life ain't ever what you figure it to be. Take that girl they was talking about on the TV just now. The one who committed suicide. I met her just once, but I used to think about her all the time. She came into the hospital when I was having my baby. Her sister was there having a baby, too, and she was visiting. But she didn't just visit her sister, she stopped into the room of all the other women having babies, talked with us for a minute, and wished us luck. People said it was just for publicity but I still think it was nice of her and I never forgot it.

Every time I'd see her in the movies or on TV she was always smiling so pretty and dressed up so nice. She was never much of an actress but it didn't matter, she had a nice personality and a pretty smile. And it used to make me think, "Lord, how lucky some people are. Look right, born right, and settled into the right profession." And I used to wonder why all of that couldn't've happened to me. Not that I ever wanted to be white or anything like that. I just wanted for once to feel like some lucky star had shined down on me. Instead of all the hardship and misery I was going through. Trouble on the job, not enough money to feed the kids, buy clothes, take care of the house, and pay the rent. Problems with Joey until he just finally packed up and left. Then trouble finding somebody to just hold me close at night. Not to marry me or anything like that. When you're a woman with two children and no husband you learn to be realistic about things like that. No, I just wanted somebody to hold me close every now and then. But even that was impossible to find. So, after the children went to sleep the nights were long. Long, long and empty. Sometimes to fill the time I'd turn on the TV and she would be in some old movie or on some talk show talking about her adventures. I remember one time she went to some country in Africa and came back with all these pictures of her with all these black folks. And I would be there and think: "This is what I want. To be rich and glamorous and to travel to all these interesting places." Her husband at that time was a photographer and I envied her that, too. The ability to meet talented, handsome men everywhere you went.

Avis was having trouble in school at this time and it seemed like every other week I had to march over to that school for one reason or another.

Then there was the time of all those problems on the job with that new supervisor who was trying to make me quit. Couldn't fire me because of the laws, but he tried so hard to make things tough for me that I would one day just up and quit. Why? I still don't know. Man just didn't like me is all I could figure. But I didn't quit. I stuck it out until one day he was the one who had to move on.

But I used to dream about what it was like being a movie actress. You don't have to worry about things like that. You make one movie, get a lot of money, and then move on to the next film. No union office to go to, no reports you have to file, no grievance committee meeting to attend. Just smile pretty for the camera and go on talk shows. Some folks just have all the luck.

Avis finally graduated, with honors of all things. And I must say I was a proud mother that day. She got herself a scholarship and is talking about going to med school. That gon' be a new money worry but I guess I will manage it.

Joey talking more about trying to be some kind of athlete. But that boy changes his mind every other month. One day it's a rap singer, other time it's a professional soldier like Colin Powell. Now it's an athlete.

Money is still tight and nights are still long, but somehow I'm getting through.

The TV said she was worried about getting old and that she ain't had a job in more than a year and a half. She saw very few men since her last divorce. And she was having all kinds of money trouble. That there was even talk abut evicting her from her apartment. The note she left said: "I'm tired, that's all. Just tired. I can't take it anymore. So I'm checking out. . . . Goodbye."

I used to think she had it golden and I had it bad. It just goes to show that you never know.

Slow Dancing with Nichelle

Donzell, twenty-six years old

Slow dancing is a thing that ain't never been outta style. Hip hop, swing, and all that other stuff is okay. But slow dancing is the thing, I don't care what nobody say.

In school we used to have these dances and the teachers would all be there just to make sure that everything stay on the up and up. And they would hire a DJ and he would play stuff and everybody would jump around and everything would be cool. And the teachers would smile at us and some of them would even dance with us if we asked them.

And then the hour would start to get late and the lights dim a little and a lot of the teachers would leave. But a few would stay. And them that stay wouldn't be paying too much attention to us anymore. And something they didn't notice, or if they did they wasn't saying anything about it, is that the music the DJ was playing was all slow stuff. The reason is because some of us guys got some money together to pay him extra for doing it.

The girls would put their head on your shoulder, and you could sometimes smell their hair and their perfume.

The one everybody liked to dance with was Nichelle because you could get in real close and as the music play and you move, you could feel all of who she was up against you. And she could feel all of who you is up against her.

Other girls would let you get close but it wasn't the same. You could feel what they had up top pressing against your chest but down below, their legs was over there and yours over here. And if you tried to get closer you just begin to stumble over each other. With Nichelle it was different. She had a way of standing with her legs wide apart that all you had to do was move in up the middle and everything was fine. And once the music start playing the two of you could move in the groove the way it supposed to be. And you never said anything while you was dancing. Too much sweet stuff was going on and your mind couldn't focus on saying any words. You was just happy to be there spending them few minutes in heaven. And when the dance was over she would just say, "Thank you. That was nice," in a whisper with a kind of a smile on her face. You weren't sure exactly what she meant, but you had a damn good idea.

All the guys used to like to dance with Nichelle but none of us ever told the other why. It was a kind of secret everybody kept to himself.

Nichelle had a boyfriend, but that didn't stop us from asking her to dance. And that didn't stop her from saying okay.

After that boyfriend she moved on to another, then another and another. One day she somehow got around to me. And you know what? . . . I married her. We been married four years now and we got us a boy and a girl.

Oh yeah, we dance together sometimes. Not a lot, but sometimes. And guess what. If the hour is right and the music is slow, I still get the same old thrill I used to get in school.

A Different World

Bob Wilson, a man in his late fifties, early sixties

You hearing that mess? Every street corner you go got one a them boys walking round. With them boom box next to him trying to give the world a headache. Some people say it's music. But to me it's noise. Just a whole lot a goddamn noise. . . . This place sure has changed. That's why I stay indoors now. I don't want to be outside dealing with stuff like that. Hell no. . . . This place sure has changed. Changed a whole lot since I used to be a young man. And it keeps changing, too. Changing for the worst, if you ask me. But I'm an old man so naturally I liked it before. When this was a different place. A different kind of world. A place where everybody used to know everybody else. Now, everybody is a stranger. And everybody's in a big hurry. Running all around the damn place. Going where? I don't know. In the old days, when one person had something to celebrate, everybody in this area used to come out and join in, make a big event for everybody to share. This place was a community. A friendly world. Put me in mind of a fellow used to live round here at the time. Undertaker named Walter Abraham. Big Abe. Everybody called him "Big Abe." A fabulous man. Loved to laugh, eat, have a good time, and dress up. Wear diamond rings on every finger. And a silk scarf round his neck. Had him this fabulous apartment there on the Boulevard. A duplex, with a staircase in the middle and windows looking out on three sides a this city. East, West, and North. Lived there with three women he told folks was his cousins. Missy, Mary, and Ruth. Everybody thought that was a lie, but nobody said anything. Hell, if a man want to have his own harem and the women want to cooperate, wasn't much left for none of us to say. More power to him. *(Pause)*

Now at the time, Big Abe was in his sixties, the women in their forties. Oh man, they went everywhere together. And every time you met them, everybody was laughing. So, whatever it is they were doing—they musta been doing right. But like I say, it wasn't any of our business. So none of us even used to speculate. . . . Anyway, Big Abe would have a party every year on his birthday. Everybody knew about it because every year he would throw open the front door and invite the whole world in. Everybody from the highest to the lowest. Everybody was welcome. There was enough liquor for an army and food to feed the city. Everybody used to look forward to Big Abe's social. It was always the social event of the year as far as we were concerned. Big time. And when he died, everybody was sorry. Broke our hearts right through. Thousands of people went to his funeral. People from everywhere, even Europe and all. He knew people from all over the world. It was the end of an era. That's what it was. The end of a whole goddamn era. Now, the city is full of punks and fools. And I got to live among them all. Listening up to all of that noise. And people want to know why I drink?

The answer, of course, is simple. . . . Ain't nothing else left to do. Know what I mean?

He takes a sip from a bottle he's carrying in a paper bag as the lights fade.

THE SORROWS OF ELVA

A MONOLOGUE PLAY IN SIX PARTS

A Fool Not to Marry

(SORROW #1)

Elva, twenty-seven years old

We met at this dance and he asked me for one. After that he kept coming back for another and another.

"Hey Elva, what is it you got that this man want so bad?" my girlfriend, Keema, asked after Louie had asked me for a fifth dance in a row.

"I don't know," I tell her, "maybe he just like the way I dance."

Keema laughed that big kinda horsey way she liked to laugh and said: "I don't think so. I think that fool in love."

"But the man just met me."

"So? That man still in love. And boy it showing all over him. You got that man in your power, girl. Anybody can see that. Anybody can see that. All they need is eyes."

Now the truth is, Louie wasn't nothing much. I mean he wasn't bad, but he wasn't nothing special. First off he was damn near thirty and I was only twenty-three. Next he didn't dress sharp or act flashy like some of the other boys I used to know and sometimes go out with. He was from the city but act like he was born in the country, if you know what I mean.

But Keema was right. That man sure was in love with me. He bought me and Keema drinks and tried to keep me in conversation most of the night. The next week he called me maybe five times asking me out. The man just wouldn't take no so finally I said yes. I let him take me out early. And sometimes after our dates when I let him kiss me goodnight at the door, I'd wait fifteen or twenty minutes till I was sure he was gone. Then I would go down to the club where Dougal was playing. He was this musician I was having a secret thing with. He was nearly forty and he smoke a lot of stuff. But he was exciting to be with in a crazy kind of way. And in the bedroom he did a lot of things boys my age didn't want to do. I mean they used to want you to do it to them, but they didn't want to do it for you. But Dougal wasn't like that. He was free, and wild. And he didn't care what he did. Especially when he was high.

But Louie kept on calling and I kept on going out with him. After a while I couldn't put him off anymore so I went back to the little room where he lived and spent the night with him.

Oh man, you would've thought I had given him the grand prize of the lottery or something. The man kept saying how much he loved me and that him and I should get married.

Married? I didn't know what he mean. He didn't have any money. I didn't have any money. What the hell was we going to get married for?

"For love," Louie said when I asked him the question. "People get married for love all the time. And after they get married, children and money come. That's how it work most of the time."

"Oh yeah?" I ask him. "Oh yeah," he said smiling that big kinda way he like to smile.

Now I don't know why but all of a sudden it sounded like a good idea. And when I mentioned it to my sister? She liked the idea, too. My mother, who never get excited about anything, said that a girl have to get married some time, sooner or later. And that it always is better sooner.

Dougal didn't get mad when I told him I was getting married and couldn't see him no more. He said it was the best thing I could do and that he was moving on anyway.

Going down to Florida to stay for a while.

We got married on a Sunday morning with my mother, my sister, my aunt, and all my friends on one side. And Louie, his brother, his mother, and some friends from his job on the other. Didn't neither of us have a father who was alive so my mother's friend, Jessie, who work for the city, give me away.

I remember just before the service I went to the bathroom to fix my dress and stuff. And for about a second in there I asked myself, "Is this what you want to do, Elva?" And I told myself, "Yes. This is exactly what you want to do. Marriage comes first. Love will come later."

Then I went out, and before God, the minister, and everybody else I said "I do" to this man I liked but didn't love. But who love me so much that everybody said I would be a fool not to marry.

Nicest Man in the World

(SORROW #2)

Elva, twenty-seven years old

"Everything is fine. Everything gon' work out." That's always the story with Louie. Everything gon' work out. All we got to do is not worry about it.

If I say, "Honey, we out of money and rent day is coming up soon," . . . "Don't worry. Everything gon' work out fine." . . . If I say, "My sister and her husband is fighting so much it look like their marriage is breaking up," "Don't worry, everything gon' work out fine." . . . If I say the elevator in this damn building is broke and one day somebody gon' get stuck in it, or might even be hurt if they don't fix it, "Don't worry, everything gon' be fine."

That man don't sing no other tune ever. If things is bad on the job. Don't worry everything gon' work out. If the Mets start losing a lot a games in a row. Don't worry, everything gon' work out.

Sometimes it make me so mad that I shout at him, "Shut up! Everything don't always work out fine unless you do something about it. Sometimes things don't even work out at all. So stop saying that, okay. Stop saying it."

And when I do that he'll look at me with that sad expression of his and say, "You right. Sometimes things don't work out. You right." And then I feel bad because I didn't mean to shout at him like that. And often things do work out. My problem is I worry too much. His problem is, he don't worry enough.

When little Scotty was born, he look like any other baby except for his eyes. I kept saying, "Louie, this child ain't right. He got a funny look in his eyes." But all he would say is "Elva, stop worrying. The child is fine." Even my mother said the same thing when I told her the child didn't look right to me. "Stop all this worrying. The child is fine. All he need is care and loving."

Well, they was wrong and I was right. Scotty got to be three and he still behave like a little infant. I took him to the hospital and they did all kinds of tests. Louie took him to the clinic and they did all kinds of therapies. I could see a little bit of improvement. But it wasn't much. That child was still running around the place hitting his face into walls and stuff.

Louie used to play with him a lot. Roll on the floor and laugh with him all the time. And everyday he would tell me the boy was improving when I knew that just wasn't true.

The woman at the clinic told us about a special program that we should send Scotty to. She even offer to write the letter for us. At first Louie didn't agree. He didn't want the boy away from us. "The child is only three. When he's four or five, if things haven't changed, then we can consider it." But I told him to hell with that. I didn't want to wait that long. So now Scotty is in that special school and we go to see him every other Saturday and Sunday.

My mother say God gives us every sorrow for a reason, but I don't see the reason for this one at all. Maybe she does, but I don't.

Louie is saying that he want us to have another child. Another cute baby. Even the doctors are saying that chances are, our next baby will be 100 percent normal. They may believe it, but I'm not sure that I do. And I don't want to bring another one like Scotty into the world.

No. Never, never again. So I told Louie that I got to think on it. I got to think on it hard and long. . . . Know what he said? "Okay, Elva, tell me when." I got to give it to him. He's a nice man. Even when he make me mad, he got to be one a the nicest men in the world.

Ain't Like It Used to Be

(SORROW #3)

Elva, twenty-seven years old

I used to see him at the hospital at least twice a week. He didn't work there but he used to come to visit and pick up that girl Nora Hansen after work. Nora was an RN and people said that she was thinking about going on and getting an MD. I didn't know her except to say hello in passing because she was working with administration. But I liked the way she dressed and carry herself. Always so groomed and proper. I used to look at her and wonder how I could be like that. Everybody respected her, even the white doctors.

When he come by to pick her up he was always dressed in a suit. He was young. Younger than her but I figured he must be some kinda executive somewhere. That's the only kind of man a woman like Nora would be seeing, I figure. People say they were planning on getting married but I didn't know for sure. Nora wasn't the kind of person to let personal information out and around the floor.

That was more'n two years ago and Nora been gone from the hospital for a while. So imagine my surprise last Sunday when I'm coming out from the supermarket and who do I see on the opposite side of the street. Josh, that guy that used to pick up Nora. I didn't really know him so I didn't say nothing to him. I just went on my way. Two blocks later I was standing there waiting on the light when he come up to me and said that my groceries was about to fall outta the bag. Then he offered to help so I told him okay.

We walked and talked and I told him his name and that I knew him from the hospital. I asked about Nora and he said he didn't know because they wasn't together anymore. I said that was a shame because they seemed like such a natural couple.

When we got to the building, I invite him up to meet Louie. For a moment he look like he wouldn't, then he said okay.

Louie invite him in and offered him beer. Then they watched some boxing together and Josh wind up staying for dinner. When he left we gave him our number and he promised he would call. That was three weeks ago.

Louie is a man who never had too many friends. Even when he was single, only person he ever hang with was his brother, Sammy. And a couple of people from his job sometimes. But most of the time he was by himself.

Me, I always had a lot of friends. Girls and boys. Then when I got married and we moved down to Manhattan, most of them people drift away. Oh, I see them every now and then, talk to one or two on the phone. But it ain't like it was before. Now it's just Louie and me and little Scotty on some weekends.

We had a nice time with Josh that night. I really thought he was going to call. But then he didn't, and I think I know why.

Something Happened

(SORROW #4)

Elva, twenty-seven years old

Something happened that wasn't supposed to happen and I don't know what to say except that it ain't gon' happen again.

I was coming outta the subway and who do I run into waiting on a train. Josh. From his expression I could tell he wasn't expecting to see me. So I asked him right out front why he didn't call. I mean we had given him dinner and everything. So I asked if my cooking was so bad that he didn't want to come back for more. I was joking but I could see he was taking it serious. He said he was busy because he was out of work and looking for a job.

"But ain't looking at night, are you?"

"No," he admit.

"Well, that's when we inviting you to come by. In the evening." After telling him that I told him to come by that Friday night around 7:30 if he had nothing to do and still remember the address. He said okay. And I told him not to BS me. If he ain't planning to make it, tell me now. He said, "Yes," he would and then I left.

When he got home I told Louie about it and about inviting Josh on Friday night. He said that was fine.

Friday night come and Louie called to say he was going to be a little late. I said okay.

Josh arrive like he said he would. He even brought a bottle of wine, which was nice. I told him about Louie being late but that I had dinner almost ready. We sat down and talked.

He told me about Nora and their breakup. He didn't say anything bad about her. Said the problem maybe was that she was too old for him. She was thirty-six and he was twenty-seven. Same age as me. I didn't realize he was that young. Dressed up in his suit like he used to be, I thought he was older. At least thirty anyway. But sitting in the living room now I could see he wasn't that old.

I asked about the kind of work he was looking for. He said he didn't know. His last job had been as a manager in some kind of warehouse and he didn't want to do that anymore.

"You used to dress so nice when you were with Nora and all," I told him. He said, "Yeah. That's when I was working for this investment firm and they was trying to make a broker out of me."

I asked what kind of work did he finally want to be doing. He said he wasn't sure, but he knew what he didn't want to do. I told him that sounded fine to me. We talked about a few other things and I said that he coulda bring his girlfriend along with him tonight. That I was cooking a whole lot of food. He said he didn't have a girlfriend. That he was right now in between. I told him I was sure he would be getting one soon. He just shrug his shoulders but didn't say anything. Then I look at the time. It was nearly nine o'clock already. Where was Louie?

We talk some more but Louie still didn't show. It wasn't like Louie to come home late on Friday nights after work. But when I thought on it, one or two times before, he had. Usually it was some boxing match or basketball he went to with his friends at work. But he didn't say nothing about that when he called.

Ten o'clock came and I couldn't wait any longer, so I told Josh that we better sit down and eat this food. He asked if he should open the wine and I said: "Why not?"

All through the dinner he looked like he was nervous, so I asked if there was anything wrong. He said no. After the meal he said, "I think I better go." I asked him why, because I was planning on making some coffee.

"It's getting late," he said.

"That ain't the reason is it?" I told him. "No," he admit. Then I told him to tell me the real reason.

"Well, it's you," he said. "I can't be in this room with you like this. Just the two of us together."

I asked him why. "Because I'm in love with you," he said. "I'm in love and I want to kiss you."

I told him to shut up. What he was saying was nonsense. He kept on saying what he was telling me was true. That he was in love with me and that was the reason why he didn't call back after he had said he would. That because of Louie and stuff the best thing to do was not to see me anymore. I told him that was a sensible idea. Then he said, "Just once. Let me kiss you just once and then I'll go."

I told him no. Then he begged me again. This time he didn't wait for my answer. He just got up close to me, put his hand on my face, and put his mouth on mine. He wasn't rough or fast, and I coulda stopped him, I'm sure. But at that moment I didn't want to. In fact my mouth opened with his and my tongue started touching his. It was then that I heard Louie's key in the door. Josh and I were in two separate parts of the room when he came in. He was smiling and said he was sorry about being late. Some man at the plant was leaving and they had a little party for him. I could see from his eyes that he was a little drunk. He kept saying to Josh, "I'm sorry man, I'm sorry. But you don't have to go. We can sit and talk a little bit."

I told him no. Told him it was late and Josh did have to go. Josh took the hint and left.

Louie, I told him he was drunk and had to get to bed. He didn't argue. He just said, "You the boss," and went in.

I did the dishes, sat on the sofa for a few minutes, turned off the lights, and went inside, too. When I got to bed, Louie was dead asleep. Of course he was, goddamn drunk.

Next morning I went by to where Josh was staying. It wasn't far. Only three blocks from where I lived. And he had given me the address the night before. He didn't have a phone so there was no way to call. But there was something about what happened and the kiss that I wanted to clear up.

He lived in this old building. Maybe the oldest building on the block.

I knocked on his door and didn't get any answer. I knocked a few more times and was about to leave when he called out, "Who is it?" I told him and he said one minute. He opened the door and didn't look too surprised. Inside after he closed the door I told him I was only staying a few minutes. He asked about Louie and I told him he was still sleeping. Then I explained that the reason I was there was so that he wouldn't get the wrong impression about the kiss and everything. That I was in love with my husband. And that if he was telling the truth about loving me, then maybe he shouldn't come by anymore. Only problem was, I didn't get a chance to say all that. The minute I started talking he was all over me kissing and touching and squeezing and whispering and putting his tongue in my ear and stuff. I tried to get him to stop but he just wouldn't. Then I started kissing him back and holding him and we fell on the bed and all kinds of exciting things start to happen. And then our clothes was in the way so we pulled them off each other. *(Pause)*

When it was over, less than an hour had passed. I couldn't believe all that had gone down in that little bit of time. He was lying on the bed kinda sleepy but smiling. I got dressed and told him I had to go. I also told him that this whole thing was a mistake and that he wasn't to see me anymore. And if he did, I would ignore him and pretend that none of this took place. He wouldn't say anything. He just repeating, "I love you . . . I love you."

I told him that was stupid and then I left.

Only a Matter of Time

(SORROW #5)

Elva, twenty-seven years old

Because I didn't believe it myself when I said it is the reason he didn't believe it either, I suppose. Because two days later, after everything I told him, Josh was on the phone telling me he want to see me, got to see me, need to see me. I hung up but he call again and again. Sometimes he call when Louie is at home and I had to pretend that I was talking to a girlfriend.

When I said I couldn't see him that boy threatened to come to the house and take off all his clothes and then mine.

The long and short of it is I went to his place and it happened again. And I enjoyed it so much that I went back again, and been going back for a little over two months now.

Since he ain't working he got all kinds a free time, so we meet twice, sometimes three times a week. If it's during the week when Louie is at work, sometimes we lay in his bed two, three hours at a time touching on each other, doing it more than once. On the weekends when we don't go to see little Scotty I sneak in an hour on Saturday and sometimes an hour on Sunday, too.

I can't lie to myself about it no more. I'm in love with Josh. Ain't nothing wrong with Louie but he just ain't the man for me. Never was. Our marriage is something other people wanted and I just went along. In bed it was okay but he never thrill me. Not in the way Josh can. Josh know things and got techniques Louie never dream about.

Plus Louie and I was never compatible in other ways. His tastes is different to mine. We couldn't even talk much because he didn't even finish high school and don't know much about anything except sports and his job. Now Josh is different. He read all kinds a stuff, even books of poetry sometimes. When I am with him it's just like not only my body opening up, but my mind, too. This is a person I want to come home to, spend all night with, and go to picnics in the park with on weekends. In other words, this is the man I want to be married to. But I haven't said none of that to Josh because I don't want to put the rush on him. I want things to take their time. Then I want him to be the one to ask me. So I'm staying on with Louie but now I know it's only a matter of time.

You know, it's funny. I feel so happy with Josh that I can't be mad at Louie anymore. I used to blame him because I was feeling unhappy. But it wasn't his fault. I married the wrong man, that's all. I married the wrong man, and he married the wrong woman. Now I feel sorry for him. And because I know we won't be together too much longer, I'm nice to him. So nice in fact that the other night I let the sex thing happen between us. I hadn't for the longest while because, well, because I just didn't want to. But now I didn't see any harm in it, so I did. And it was okay.

Josh never ask if I do it with Louie, and when I try to tell him, he say he don't want to know.

Sometimes I ask him about Nora and what it was like laying up in bed with her like he is with me. But he won't talk about that either. All he will say is he don't remember. I know he remember but he just won't talk about it. Maybe he feel that it ain't none of my business. And that's okay. I even respect him for it.

The room he live in ain't much. It's even worse than our place because the bathroom is down the hall. But I love it because of what it mean to him and me. Us. I think about us getting married and living there for a little while, then moving out. Maybe moving to another project.

Everybody say I'm looking better and smiling more. Even Louie been saying that. If it's true, I know why, of course. Only problem is, I can't say nothing about it. Not until the time is right anyway.

So I'm sitting here and smiling because I have a secret. I know something they don't know. And I'm holding it close. Close inside me. And everyday it get bigger and bigger. And one day it'll get so big that it'll just burst out. And that's the day everybody will know.

Dreams Die First

(SORROW #6)

Elva, twenty-seven years old

"A husband and a wife is only part of the plan. Put a baby in their hands and you have the family of man." I used to hear that said when I was a kid. And I guess I believed it, which is maybe why I got married as young as I did.

Today it seem like I don't have one child but three. Scotty, my natural one, Louie, who sometimes act like a child, and Josh, who now is beginning to. He started acting moody and pouty and spiteful and stupid. Why? I don't know. Everything between us was going along okay. And I never put any pressure on him or anything like that. I never even told him about all the dreams and plans I had for us being together all the time. Those dreams they used to see me through the day and night. And made it possible for me to live with Louie the way I was. I figured that when the time was right it would just all fall together naturally. Plus I didn't want to scare him off. Some men, when they hear you got plans, the first thing they do is to start looking for some window or back door to sneak out of. I seen it before. And I even used to hear them talk about it when I was single. So I wasn't going to make that mistake. I ain't that dumb.

Josh and I had a routine and I stuck to it. In fact it got so regular that after a while when I got to his place we didn't have to do too much talking. I would say hello, make sure the door was closed, and start taking my clothes off. And since we didn't go out anywhere, there wasn't much sense in sitting around with my dress on. Plus it was more comfortable.

In the beginning he was so excited and eager that he would be all over me just as I walk, sometimes forgetting to close the door behind us. Which is why I like to check it before I start anything.

But now things have changed a little bit. When I come in he's laying on the bed. I take off my clothes and he still on the bed. I join him, we talk, or listen to the radio. And then after that is when we turn to each other, touch a little bit and start.

I know what you're saying. He's getting used to me. Sure. And I'm getting used to him, too. And that's nice. Two people together for a while can't always act like they just met each other. They get into routines. They get into patterns. And that's how it was with Josh and me. I got nothing against patterns. Patterns is the story of life.

But Josh started to get moody. For no reason at all he would snap at me. Other times he would criticize what I was wearing, and how I talk even. I know I'm not as educated as him, but I'm not dumb either. I read books and magazines. I listen to news reports and look at PBS sometimes. I look at talk shows, too. In fact, I look at them a lot when I'm home during the week. I told him so, and you know what he said to me? He said, "Talk shows is for fools." So I asked him straight up, "You calling me a fool?" He said, "No, I'm just stating a fact, that's all." Then he didn't say anything more.

I went home and I thought about it all night and even into the next day. I thought about it so much that the next night Louie asked me if there was anything wrong. I told him no, and he went back to looking at the TV.

The next time I went to see Josh I didn't take my dress off. I just closed the door behind me and looked at him for the longest while. "What's the matter?" he asked me. I told him nothing and everything. When he said he didn't understand, I told him we couldn't see each other no more. When he asked why, I told him it was because he wasn't respecting me. And that he was bored with me, too. I told him about all the plans I had for us getting married and stuff. Told him about wanting to be with him ever since I used to see him at the hospital with Nora. "I used to love you and I still do. And maybe to your mind I don't know a lot. But I do know that love without respect don't mean a thing."

He lay on the bed but he didn't say nothing. I think he was a little dumbstruck. Maybe he wasn't, but he didn't talk. So I turned around and left.

It wasn't until I was a few blocks away that my chest start to hurt and my eyes start to fill. So I went into the park and sat on a bench by myself. A whole bunch of people passed by but I wasn't seeing them. All I could see were some kids in a playground playing. Some years ago I had read a book called *Dreams Die First*. I didn't know what the title meant then, but I sure knew it now. You see, with all the things I said to Josh, the one thing I didn't mention was the fact that I was pregnant. With his baby. No, I didn't mention that at all.

Two nights later while we were sitting around having dinner I said to Louie that I thought I was pregnant.

"You serious?" he asked. And when I told him yes, the smile on his face got as big and round as the moon.

The baby was born and we calling her Louisa. The doctors say that she's healthy and normal in every way. Louie is like a man who won the Powerball lottery over and over. And every time he pick her up, you know what he say to me? "You see what I told you, Baby? Everything gon' work out fine."

RAP TALK

The Professor

The professor is in his late teens/early twenties and wears a grad cap and gown as well as eyeglasses.

I am the professor, perhaps you heard.
I am the one who looks like a nerd.
But looks are deceiving, believe you me
'Cause what I've got to
Say you better take seriously.
Your body may be the temple
Of your soul
But your mind is what keeps
It in control.
So what I'm here to talk
About is your spine and your brain
And I'm going to keep going
Back to it again and again.
Laugh if you want to,
But it's at your expense
'Cause if you get
Brain damage, you won't be able to
Make any sense
Of your dreams, desires, your future, or your life
And all your living days will be caught up in the strife
Of depending on others for what you used to do
Like eating your food and going to the bathroom, too.
I'm not here to threaten
And I don't aim to scare
All that I want to do is
Make you aware

That brain and spinal injury
Is something to take seriously
Because it's taking its toll
Nationally.
Here are some facts you may not know
So we're going to give them
To you and we're going to do it slow.
No rhythm, no rap, no groovy
Dance movement
Just some straight info for
Your health improvement.
So listen up!

He goes to a chart where the facts are written and points them out.

Here we go: National Facts About Brain Injury.

Fact One: A brain injury occurs every fifteen seconds in the United States.

Fact Two: 75,000 to 100,000 people die every year from brain injuries. And that figure is rising.

Fact Three: In the past twelve years, more people have died of brain injuries than in all American-fought wars since the founding of the United States. Wow. That's a lot of people.

Fact Four: The majority of brain injuries occur in the 10 to 35 age group. With the highest peak between 15 and 25 years of age. Fifteen and twenty-five. That's where most of us fit.

The principal causes of brain and spinal injury are: motor vehicle–related accidents. Speeding, reckless driving, driving while under the influence of drugs, booze, or other kinds of distractions.

Falls. Out of trees, off of diving boards or bicycles, skateboards, buildings, etc.

Don't misunderstand me. I'm not saying you can't do all these things. I'm just saying be careful.

And use common sense. Wear helmets, seatbelts, and don't take foolish risks.

And don't forget about intentional injury. Yes. Fighting. Violence. Beating each other up whether it's one on one or gang related. It'll cost you big time so let it go.

He goes back to his rap.

Now you have all the facts and you have all the info
I don't plan on saying any mo'.
But even if you forget them all, remember this for me:
That prevention is the key
To avoiding brain and spinal injury.

PREVENTION!

The Other Me

Vinette, in her early twenties, is sitting in a wheelchair.

There is another me inside what you see
A dancing girl who wants to be free
But a foolish dive took it all away from me.
The situation went like this:
I was out with some friends and we did this thing
It was just for a joke, kinda as a fling.
We went to this girl's house
While her parents were away
And asked her to come out and hang,
Come out and play.
She said she couldn't because it was late
But said we could party
In the house, and we said, "Great."
So we called up some guys,
And other friends from the hood,
Told them to bring drinks
And stuff to make the party good.
About thirty people showed up for our midnight event
Including Bobby, Billy, Barbie,
Lucy, Annie, Davey, and Brent.
The music was so loud a neighbor came to scold
But we told her she was jealous because
We were young and she was old
Then we back inside to laugh
It up some more.
Bobby was the one who had the
Idea for a swim

I said "sure" and made a bet that I'd beat him in.
He ran fast but I ran faster
Not realizing for a moment that I was racing toward disaster.
The pool had been emptied but I couldn't tell
It was so dark that I dived right into hell.
My body must've twisted before I hit the deck
Because the injury wasn't to my head but to my neck.
Now I can sit here, talk, smile, and frown
But I have no control of my body from my shoulders down.
The rest of me might as well be dead
Because what I've become is a talking head.
People or machines do everything for me, even breathe.
You wouldn't believe what a big deal
It is for me to get something to read.
So I sit here and think of my life before that dive
And all the schemes and dreams I used to contrive
Are no more.
Something else replaces them.
Medicine, drugs, therapy, and hope.
Hope for a medical breakthrough,
Hope for a miracle.
And while I sit here and wait
I convince myself that:
There is another me inside what
You see.
A dancing girl who is athletic
And free.
She didn't make that dive, she
Didn't even go out that night
And everything in her life is coming out all right.
So don't be fooled by what you see here
The real me is that person dancing
Over there.

Lights up on another girl dressed in the same outfit dancing and moving to music. They turn and look at each other. Lights fade.

I Used to Be Cool

A young man somewhere between the ages of seventeen and twenty-five years old comes out in a wheelchair; wheels around an empty stage for a while; makes a few attempts to rise out of the chair, but discovers that he can't. Finally, he settles in and accepts his condition. Slowly, he wheels himself toward the audience and begins to speak.

I still think I'm dreaming
Because I used to be cool.
I was hip to the new dances
I was nobody's fool.
Chicks used to come on to me
Everywhere I'd go.
Guys used to envy me
Because I was the guy to know.

Then one night some buddies
And me
Decided to drink ourselves stupid
Just to see
Who was real macho
And who was a clown
Who could stand up to his liquor
And who would have to lay down.

So, I downed the stuff hard
And I downed it fast
And though they were trying to
Keep up

Rap Talk

I knew they couldn't last.

Whiskey, scotch, rye, bourbon, and gin
Rum, tequila, vodka, and beer
I took them all in.

The guys were all trying
But they couldn't keep the pace
I was all the way out front
In this alcohol race.

Finally, Bobby said: "Hey, man, I'm done,"
And the others guys finally admitted
That I won.

Everybody was stumbling
Some wanted to barf
All I could do was sit there and laugh.

Now they knew who "El Jefe" was—
Who was the "Daddy."
I was the "golfer"
And they were the "caddie."

Then it was time to go home
And Bobby said, "Don't drive."
I looked at that fool trying
To hand me that jive.
I can drink and drive
Because I am in control.
Not of the liquor or the car,
But of my mind and my soul.
You just get in the car
And turn the key like so.

I Used to Be Cool

And when you hear the
Engine buzzing
Just go with the flow.

An engine starts up.

That's what I did
and everything was groovy
it was like a scene in a racing car movie.

I was turning up that highway
Just feeling free
Then for no reason at all there
Was this rock and this tree
Then this bush and this mountain
Coming fast at me.

It all happened in one big flash.
And the next thing I heard was
This incredible crash.

Sirens and red lights and people
Running all around
But for some strange reason I
Couldn't hear a sound.
It was like being in a silent movie
Or in a weird dream
And all I wanted to do was
Jump up and scream:
"Help me! Help me! I need to
cough—there's a car on my
chest and I can't get it off."

People told me later that I was in a haze

And this condition of mine went
On for days.

Doctors, lawyers, parents, friends,
And insurance people, too,
All came to see me to figure out what
To do.
Mother cried and Dad said, "We'll make it, son."
That's easy for him to say because
He ain't the one
Who's tied to this chair, who
Can't get up and run.

Despair is what you think of
When you're in this state.
You want to change things
But realize it's too late.
Too late to go back and say
"Stop me, I'm a fool."
Because all the things I was doing
I thought made me cool.
I still think I'm dreaming
But it's a dream gone bad
Like it's the worst nightmare
Anybody's ever had.
My life was changed
All my friends are gone
And this wheelchair and
Me will go on and on.

I'm in rehab now and things
Are getting better.
They're teaching me to cope
And what that means is that there is hope

Of a new life and new adventures.
So, I'm going to try.

"It ain't over till it's over,"
Yogi Berra used to say.
And with that thought in mind, I'll be on my way.

Just one more thing before I go.
Don't Drink and Drive. It'll cost
You. Believe me, I know.

He wheels off to the nearest exit.

Andy's Rap

Andy, twenties

Looka here, looka here, don't you be no square.
Come see what I'm selling right in here.
I got dresses and shoes and pretty bow ties.
Catch all them foxes big brown eyes.
This stuff is new and that ain't no joke.
And with the prices I'm charging you'll never go broke.
I got dream sights too, if you know what I mean.
When the world start to look ugly I can make it all clean.
Suppose your old lady getting down on your ass.
Say you got no ambition and no goddamn class.
Don't beat up the bitch or blow out your brain.
Just come see me man, and I'll make it all sane.
24 hours I'm open and ready.
Got all the powdery stuff to keep you steady.
Send you to stars you never dreamed about.
Just when it look like things was really down and out.
Don't take the train, a plane, or no boat.
I's got the stuff to keep you afloat.
Paradise ain't about going to church and dying.
Come see me in here and I'll send you out flying.
And if you never frown.
You got a real treat coming.
Don't wait another day,
Come in and start humming.
Now, I know what you heard about just saying "No"
But when the pain get too bad, you got to "go with the flow"
So, take a look at me, I'm steady and cool.

Andy's Rap

The man can't make me no 9-to-5 fool.
What I'm telling you ain't no lie.
Come in an' sample the goods.
Don't even have to buy.
Who gon' be first, now don't be shy.
You know you want to.
Just come in and try.
Come on . . . Be brave . . .

The American Tradition

This rap can be done by a girl or a guy.

Now listen here and listen up good.
I'm going to shout this out all over the hood.

I'm talking about slavery
A real bad condition
Which used to be a part of
The American tradition.

They would catch you, break you,
And put you in chains
Crush you under their boots like
You didn't have any brains.

It started in the old world then moved on to the new
Where they built a whole economy on slave revenue

They would catch them in Africa
And put them on a ship
Then beat them and starve them
For the whole trip.
Now when they reached the New World they were auctioned
on the block
Where people bought and sold them to increase their stock.

The father to this farm, the mother over there
With the baby in the middle, didn't nobody care.
A slave is a slave, you can take it from me

All this was a part of American history.

That's right, a slave was a slave,
That was his condition
And it all was a part
Of the American tradition.

The American tradition
The American tradition
The American tradition
Oh yeah.

Now there used to be a person called "The Auctioneer."
That man bought and sold black folks everywhere.
He would take slaves and put them up on a stand
And the people would make bids by raising their hand.

Let me now give you an example of what you would see
In this place we now call "The Land of Democracy."

(*As the auctioneer*)

Let's get it together
Ain't got no time to waste
Come get your slave purchased
And let's do it with haste.
I got big ones, small ones,
Fat ones and lean
And all the other sizes
That come in between.

Just show me your money
And you can take your pick
Don't just stand there staring

Like you is some hick.

Check them out close
And see what you like
'Cause if you ain't spending
You gonna have to take a hike.

See this one here, he is a good-looking feller
You can work him in the fields or in your cellar.
And this pretty one here, I don't have to tell you what she
can do.
You got an imagination, so it's all up to you.
And babies, babies, babies,
I got babies galore
Bring 'em up anyway you like
And they'll make you happy for sure.

Money talks. Ain't nothing for free
But everything I sell, I guarantee.
Give me your hand, I'll show you the way
To get very rich in America today.

The condition of slavery was real, real mean
And it was all a part of the American scene.

We black and free they tell us now
But we still a bunch a second-class citizens somehow.
And it look like the situation gon' always be
That we gon' always have to fight to keep ourselves free

'Cause we never want to go back to that old condition
That used to be a part of the American tradition
Oh nooooo—

FIVE BLACK HEROES IN MONOLOGUES

Frederick Douglass (1818–1895)

Born Frederick Augustus Washington Baily in Baltimore, Maryland, Douglass was a slave who escaped, changed his name, and went on to be the most articulate and passionate spokesman of the antislavery movement. He was an abolitionist, a newspaper editor, a public speaker of renown, a politician (he once ran for Vice President of the United States), and an author. He wrote three autobiographies: *Narrative Life of Frederick Douglass, My Bondage and My Freedom* and *Life and Times of Frederick Douglass*. In 1877, President Rutherford B. Hayes made him the Marshall of the District of Columbia. And in 1889 he was appointed Minister and Consul General to Haiti. He was also known as an outspoken champion of women's rights.

I Will Raise Both My Hands

Frederick Douglass, in his fifties, stands at a podium dressed in period garb.

There is a story about two poisonous snakes. One's facing north, the other facing south. One's name is Freedom, the other: Slavery. Both bit the Negro and both bites were bad. . . . The Civil War was over but our battle had just begun.

No sooner had the war ended than the Southern states began enacting "black codes" and "penal laws" to return the freed slaves to the control of their former masters. Mississippi prohibited black men from owning or even renting land. South Carolina and other states were forcing black women and men to work as hired farm hands or domestics for cruelly low wages or face arrest as vagrants. The employers had the power to starve black people to death and that, to my mind, was still the power of slavery. Under these conditions, what does freedom mean?

I thought about it, then thought about it some more. And although officially retired, I had to speak my piece. *(Moving to center stage)*

Slavery is not abolished until the black man has the ballot. While the Legislature of the South retains the right to pass laws making any discrimination between black and white, slavery still lives there.

If the Negro knows enough to fight for his country, he knows enough to vote. If he knows enough to pay taxes, he knows enough to vote.

The government think it's done enough for the slaves by freeing them, but this freed slave is still a slave to society. If a man can't vote or exercise his rights as a citizen, what's the purpose of his being free in a democracy? If the black man is to have any hope of surviving he must be given the ballot now.

The sound of applause as Douglass goes back to his desk.

As I traveled the country agitating for the vote opposition came from a very curious place. Here is a letter I received from Elizabeth Cady Stanton.

"Dear Mr. Douglass,

The representative women of this nation have done their utmost for the last thirty years to secure freedom for the Negro. Now that this has been achieved, what about women's rights? The old antislavery school says that women must stand back until the rights of Negroes are recognized. But on this question of suffrage I say, if you will not give the whole loaf to the entire people, then give it to the most intelligent first. Women."

I could not agree and told her so. I explained that the cause of Negro suffrage was more urgent to me because Negroes were being lynched, shot, castrated, and burned at the stake. We need the vote for our protection.

When women, because they are women, are dragged from their homes and hung upon lampposts, and when their children are torn from their arms, then they will have the urgency to obtain the ballot ahead of the black man.

We battled this issue in public and in private. And this battle was especially painful to me because it put me at odds with so many women whom I had respected and admired. Women like Harriet Beecher Stowe, Elizabeth Cady Stanton, and Susan B. Anthony. But I could not be stopped and would not be stopped. There was too much at

stake for the black man at this juncture. And then finally
. . . finally it came to pass *(He reads from a document):*

Fourteenth Amendment
No state shall make or enforce any laws which shall
abridge the privileges or immunities of citizens of the
United States nor shall any state deprive any person of life,
liberty or property without due process of law, nor deny
any person within its jurisdiction the equal protection of
the laws. Ratified July 21, 1868.

He reads from another document.

Fifteenth Amendment
The rights of the citizens of the United States to vote shall
not be denied or abridged by the United States or by any
state on account of race, color or previous condition of
servitude. Ratified March 30, 1870.

The battle, on paper at least, was won. But how expensive
was the cost? I wondered if I could now reach out the arm
of friendship and be thus embraced by those who through
necessities of their own had been made opponents to our cause.

He rises.

I am happy to say, it was. And I was once again invited to
the platforms where women's rights were being champi-
oned.

Douglass moves to center stage.

Man in his arrogance has hitherto felt himself fully equal to
the work of governing the world without the help of women.

He has kept the reins of power securely in his own hands, and the history of nations and the present experience of the world show the woeful work he has made of governing.

The slaveholders used to represent the slaves, the rich landowners in other countries represent the poor, and the men in our country claim to represent women. But the true doctrine of American Liberty plainly is that each class and each individual of a class should be allowed to represent themselves.

The right of women to vote is sacred in my judgment. And if called upon to give my assent in any official capacity I will raise both my hands in its favor. And this is a right that should be given as quickly as possible.

Slavery of one kind has ended, but another continues. So long as women are refused the right to vote they are enslaved. Therefore, I urge you to petition your Congressmen and Representatives on this important subject. For the sooner women are allowed to vote, the sooner America will truly be the land of the free.

Are we free, I wonder. Will we ever be truly free? Or is freedom an abstraction that can never be made into a practical reality? I sometimes think I know. But often times I'm baffled. Yet of this much I'm sure. Freedom, whether an abstraction or a fact, is something worth fighting for. So the battle continues.

Lights fade slowly as Douglass goes back to his writing.

Mahalia Jackson (1911–1972)

Born in New Orleans, Louisiana, and raised on the banks of the Mississippi Delta, Mahalia Jackson was perhaps the greatest gospel singer America has ever known. Almost single-handedly she brought black gospel music from the churches of Chicago to the capital cities of the world. She sang at Carnegie Hall and the White House, and sold millions and millions of records. All during her forty-five-year career Mahalia fought and campaigned for the rights of African Americans through her activities and through her music.

Why I Sing Gospel

Mahalia Jackson, fifty-nine or sixty years old

A bare stage with one chair off to the side. Bessie Smith's record-ing of "I Hate to See That Evening Sun Go Down" is heard in the background. Mahalia, who's sitting, is listening to it. She hums along and picks up on the vocal for a few bars, then begins to speak as the music fades out.

People always asking me why I only sing gospel. Some even went so far as to try and tempt me with money and other stuff if I would sing jazz or blues. But I ain't ever slipped, and I ain't ever wavered. Gospel is my music and gospel is what I sing.

Now to me the greatest blues singer who ever lived was Bessie Smith. And as a child I used to listen to her records whenever I could and try to imagine what it must be like to open my mouth and make the kind of music that could reach the hearts and minds of so many people. I used to image it and dream it, but the blues wasn't for me. I wasn't born to that kind of rhythm. Our Baptist church didn't have no organ and no trumpets or no piano neither. Just a preacher saying words with the faithful clapping hands and humming and a true saved sister beating on a tambourine.

In the distant background we hear humming and a tambourine. Mahalia listens for a moment and begins to clap her hands in time.

That was the music that stirred my blood and fired my soul. That's the music that set my heart to singing and it ain't stopped yet. And I ain't stopped neither. Gospel been good to me and I ain't got no reason not to be faithful. People say to me all the time, "Oh Halia, because of you America is singing gospel music in the morning, singing it at Christmas time. And singing it, too, in times of trials and tribulations. You have made gospel music a part of our lives." . . . They tell me that all the time. And I admit I had a hand in it. Oh yes, a big hand. But Halia ain't the only one. No sir, not at all. Right now there are more than eight hundred gospel singing groups touring and playing to packed churches and concerts all over this country. The Lord God Almighty has always been popular. I am just but one voice carrying his word. . . . Still others ask: "Why do you just sing gospel? Why don't you sing other music, too?"

Well, I've tried to answer that over and over. Let me see if I can by telling you a little story.

Some years ago I met a young man. He was a talker and a dreamer. And he could make the rocks move and the oceans swell with the sound of his voice and the power of his words. His name was Martin King. Martin Luther King. A young man from Georgia who loved his Mama's cooking and some lively music when he was worshipping his Maker. We used to talk all the time and he used to ask me to sing all the time. Then our paths got separated. His business took him in one direction, my business took me in another. I started out in Chicago, moved on to New York and Carnegie Hall, and then on to Paris, London, Germany, and all over the world. Then after I got sick I had to come back home and settle down quiet for a while. . . . That was the Lord telling me I was doing too much, and pushing this tired body a little too hard. . . . Oh, I wasn't ready to give up or nothing like that. No, I was just going to sit in my kitchen and let things take their own time as far as career and future was concerned.

And I was doing just that. Cooking and spending time with family and friends. Making a few recordings when the spirit moved me. Even went to Hollywood and made me a movie during this time. Noo, I didn't act no part. I was singing. Singing the word of the Lord up on that big silver screen. So like I was saying, everything was quiet and fine. Then one day I got a call. It was from Martin, who I hadn't seen in a number of years. He was calling to invite me to this march he was organizing—this march to the Lincoln Memorial in Washington, DC. Now I had been to Washington a couple of years before. John Kennedy had asked me to sing at his inauguration, and that was some honor for a little girl born by a river in New Orleans, Louisiana. But to be invited to this event by Mr. King was an even bigger honor.

"Halia," he said to me, "I got a special favor to ask. . . . I want you to sing. I want you to sing like you never sung before. The date is August 28. The place is Washington, DC. . . . I want you to go out there before I speak. I want you to calm them down for me. Think you could do that?"

"I'll certainly try," I told him. "I'll certainly try."

The morning was overcast and the advance word was that not many people would show up. They expected only a few hundred. Then around eleven the sun came out and the people began to pour in. Not by the tens or hundreds, but by the thousands and thousands. Well, over a quarter of a million was there. And it wasn't just black folks. White folks, green folks, red folks, and blue folks. All kinds of people. And the time came for me to sing. And for the first time in I don't know how many years, I was nervous. Really, really nervous. Everything was so quiet. . . . Everybody was just standing there waiting. All those millions of people.

Pause. By this time she should be standing looking at an empty spotlight center stage.

I opened my mouth and the words started to come.

We hear her recording of "I've Been Buked and I've Been Scorned."

Then all in a flash it was over. The place explodes like thunder. I didn't know where I was. Somebody led me off the stage. Then Martin went out and spoke.

Pause. As in the background we hear the end of MLK's "I Have a Dream" speech.

After that speech, if I didn't know before, I knew then why I had to sing gospel. And why I am going to go on singing it right to the end of my days.

We hear the sound of another Mahalia Jackson recording as she stands there listening and the lights begin to fade.

Charles "Buddy" Bolden (1877–1931)

Bolden is a figure shrouded in fact and legend. Considered to be "The First Man of Jazz," or more accurately, the first musician to give jazz (or *jass* as they called it in those days) widespread popularity, Buddy Bolden's story is curious. For a man who is credited as the father of an important musical movement and as a person who was extremely popular (for a short time [1900–1905]), virtually nothing was written about him. All that is known is that he was born in New Orleans in 1877, played the cornet, was the first popular jazz musician anyone could remember, was diagnosed as insane in 1907, and spent the last twenty-four years of his life institutionalized. He died in 1931 at age fifty-four unaware that the "jassy" music he'd just about invented had flourished and developed into America's most indigenous art form.

My Own Private Blues

Buddy Bolden at twenty-six

Bolden is sitting on a chair with a bottle on the floor and his cornet next to it. He's been indoors for three days and looks somewhat disheveled.

People is starting to copy the way I play. All over town you hear them talking 'bout Buddy Bolden kinda music. King Bolden music. And every damn musician that hear us steal something. That's all they come by now to do. Steal. This is turning out to be a city full of thieves and all you can tell me is to pay them no mind? They taking the food from my table and the music from my horn and I don't know what to do about it. I could bust somebody's face and kick somebody's butt, and that's what I'm going to do if it don't stop. Yeah, that's what I'm going to do.

He takes a long drink from the bottle, sits and thinks for a little. Begins to sing softly.

> Thought I heard Buddy Bolden say
> We need a new kind of music.
> Take the old stuff away
> Rag it up, jass it up
> Take it away
> Yeah—that's what Mr. Bolden say.

Hattie had the baby. Refused to let me see it, can you believe that. I can't see my own baby. Say I'm a no-account, no-char-

acter lowlife who don't deserve to have no child. Say she
don't want the boy growing up like me. I tried to see him
over and over again but every time I get close to the house
something stop me. I don't know what it is, but this thing,
this power stop me, and I can't get any closer. I try and this
thing push me back. I mean hard. It push me back hard.

I know you don't believe me. Or maybe you think it's
the liquor talking. But it's true. I swear to God, it's true.
What you don't know, you see . . . What you don't know is
that Hattie got powers. Voodoo powers she bring from up
the river. Powers she get from her grandmother. She told
me so. Said she was going to put a spell on the house and a
spell on me, too. Other people tell me she been working
on it every time she get a chance. When we was together
she was always doing stuff on other people. I used to pay it
no mind, but now she turning it on me. . . . That's why
everybody stealing my music. That's why I'm having trouble playing it, too. You didn't know that. I didn't tell you. I
went in the other day to practice with the boys. Nothing
big, just wanted to try a couple new tunes. It was like I
never played before. Every note come out wild and wrong.
The harder I tried the worst it got. After a while Lou said
it was no use, we better call it a day. I told him it was
Hattie, she is the one putting a spell on me. He wouldn't
believe it. Lou never want to believe anything he can't
touch or see. Said I was tired because I was up and drinking all night. I been up and drinking for three days and
three nights, he didn't know that. But it don't affect me
that way. I could always play the horn. I can always make
the music happen. That's why they call me King
Bolden. . . . No, no. This was the first time and I know it
got something to do with Hattie. I don't care what nobody
say, I know that for a fact. *(Takes another drink)*

I'm starting to get them headaches again and all that

stuff the doctor give me ain't helping. Only thing that helps is taking a lot of this stuff and going to sleep. And staying asleep until the devil stop stomping around in my head. I tell that to the boys but they don't understand. They think I'm jiving. Think I'm using it as an excuse not to show up. Lou say Sam is upset and talking about not wanting to give me my share. But I am the band. The band is me. Even when I ain't there I's the one the people come to see. I's the reason the band even got any booking. They just jealous that's all. Jealous because I'm the one everybody come to hear. Not Jimmy, not Willie, not Jeff or Lou—Me. King Bolden—me.

I ain't been outta this room for three days, you know why? Mama say there's a man with a gun looking for me. Man say I do it with his wife and give her the disease, she do it with him, now he got the disease. So he blame me. Only one thing wrong. I don't know the man or his wife. So that man blaming me for something I ain't done. Got enough trouble with the women around me, don't need to go after no stranger. Especially no married stranger. But that man don't want to hear. Mama tried to talk to him, but he wasn't listening. Got only one thing in mind. Want to put a bullet in the heart of the man he think ruined his wife.

I ain't going out. If it take forever, I ain't going out. Let him kill another Buddy Bolden. Got a whole lot of other Charles Boldens in New Orleans. Let him kill one a them and let me be.

You the only one I can talk to. The only one I can trust. You think I'm wrong wanting to see my son? Everybody get to pick their boy up, hold him in their arms, and look at the smile on his face. Why can't I be the same? Why do I have to have a woman who hate me putting spells every place I go?

The music I play, they call it ratty music, darkie music, lowdown music, noisy music, no music. Now everybody want to take it and claim it for their own.

He takes another drink and begins to sing again.

I thought I heard Buddy Bolden say
da, da, da, da, da, da, da, etc. *(Stops singing)*

You think this is the end of me, don't you? Think you seeing the finish of buddy Bolden, the King. You wrong, pal. You wronger than wrong. This is just the beginning of a new season and a new day. The music gon' flow, the sun gon' be shining, and all the people gon' be out there laughing and eating and listening to all that music. And I'm going to be there, playing up a storm. Oh yeah, I'm going to be blowing like I never blowed before. And you know what the people gon' say? "Oh, that's just Buddy calling his children home. Buddy the King, blowing his self out through that horn."

Yeah, that's what they're going to say when they hear me play again. . . . Yeah that's exactly what they're going to say.

He goes back to the bottle, takes a long sip as the lights fade.

Coretta Scott King (1927–)

Mrs. Martin Luther King was born in Marion, Alabama. In 1951, she received a bachelor's degree (B. S.) from Antioch College in Antioch, Ohio, and a bachelor's degree in music (Mus. B.) from the New England Conservatory of Music in Boston.

Coretta Scott made her concert debut as a singer in Springfield, Ohio, in 1948. She then gave numerous performances in the United States as well as in India. She was married to the civil rights leader in 1953.

During her married years with MLK she maintained the stability of their family life and actively supported his civil rights initiatives. After his death, she has vigorously continued to be active in the civil rights movement, becoming the president of the Martin Luther King Memorial Center and joining the board of directors of the Southern Christian Leadership Conference. She wrote an autobiography in 1969, *My Life with Martin Luther King.*

Coretta Remembers

Coretta Scott King

The memory is an impolite intruder who hides itself in the attic of your mind and chooses to come out only at the most inconvenient moments. When you're standing on the street waiting for a bus to come. Or when you're listening to someone and a word they say or phrase they use reminds you of someone or a time long ago. Sometimes it gets triggered by the words of a song or the sound of a special voice.

Time sometimes heals wounds, but it can never replace the loved ones that we've lost. So we're left with memories of the times we spent together. The good and the bad. And those rare quiet moments in between. *(Pause)*

With the passage of time, Martin has become as controversial in death as he was in life. There are many who will question, distort, exploit, and impugn what he stood for and what he accomplished. We who were close to him know the man he was and we hold his memory dear.

Perhaps for me the happiest memory I have of Martin is in 1964 when we went to Oslo, Sweden, for him to accept his Nobel Prize. Although we knew he had been nominated, his getting it came as a complete surprise.

"This year the prize is worth 54,000 dollars," the reporter said to him. "What do you intend to do with the money, Mr. King?"

"Divide it among the Southern Christian Leadership Conference, the Congress of Racial Equality, the Student Non-Violent Coordinating Committee, the NAACP, the

National Council of Negro Women, and the American Foundation on Non-Violence," he answered. *(Pause)*

The prize was important for it said that Martin's activities were recognized as worthwhile not just here in America, and not just among African American peoples, but by everyone, the world over.

Privately, I was pleased because it told our four children better than I could ever imagine that their father, who had been jailed so many times, and had been called *a liar, a communist, an Uncle Tom, a criminal,* and every other unpleasant name one could think of, had been right after all. And the rightness of his stand had now been universally recognized.

There were so many events and ceremonies to attend. All required formal wear and Martin who had been such a dandy when I first met him found it annoying having to wear a bow tie. The problem was, he didn't know how to tie it.

"Why do I have to wear one of these? Why can't I wear the clip-on kind?" he asked. I explained in formal wear this was the only kind that was acceptable. . . . "This thing is a pain. It always comes out looking lopsided. The clip-on kind is neat and it's no bother to wear." . . . Finally, I said, "Let me." And I tied it for him. Then he wanted to know: "How'd you learn to tie these things? Have you been sneaking off behind my back taking lessons?" And we laughed. Then he said, "Let's take a quiet moment to reflect how long and how difficult it's been for us to get to this place." We hugged and then we cried a little because I guess somewhere inside we knew we'd never have a moment like that again.

Then with his tie straight and a special flower given to him by the children he went to accept that great honor. He accepted the prize on behalf of the twenty-two million black people in America who were engaged in a mighty battle to end the long night of racial injustice. "I accept this award," he said, "with an abiding faith in America, and an audacious faith in the future of mankind."

Martin is gone but the faith he inspired endures. And so do we. Thank you for coming here tonight. And God bless you all.

She exits.

James Baldwin (1924–1987)

James Baldwin was a writer in the fullest sense of the word. He wrote novels, poems, plays, screenplays, essays, and a children's book. He was and is still regarded as one of the best writers America has produced in the latter half of the twentieth century. Best known for his essays, James Baldwin became the window through which white America could view the fire and the passion of the black man's soul.

I met James Baldwin in 1985, at Virginia Commonwealth University, right after I had adapted his novel, *Go Tell It on the Mountain,* for a PBS TV movie. He was pleased with the adaptation and with the end result. He was on a lecture tour. We appeared on stage together, had lunch and drinks together, and talked. We discussed the possibility of adapting some of his other works for media, but this never came to pass. When he died it was said that we will never see his like again. His work endures but he is still missed.

A Dream of Deliverance

James Baldwin, in his thirties

I was asked to come here to speak and the subject, of course, is to be my life. My life as it relates to my writing. But to talk about my writing I must talk about America. And to talk about America I must talk about race and race relations. How it has stunted and crippled the potential of this great nation. And how it will go on crippling it until we come to our senses. Some time ago I said that the American black person is a part of this country. And the day we face up to that fact is the day we will become a nation. Maybe even a great one.

I believed it then and despite evidence to the contrary, I believe it now. You see I was born in the church. Gospel and prayers and optimism have always been a part of my psychic condition. So I am hopeful about America and dream of its deliverance.

As I said, I was born in Harlem but ended up in France. I started out with gospel but moved on to the blues. I said *Go Tell It on the Mountain* and offered my *Notes of a Native Son*, warned about *The Fire Next Time*, moved to *Another Country* due to the *Evidence of Things Not Seen*.

Stood in the *Amen Corner* and sang the *Blues for Mr. Charlie*. *One Day When I Was Lost*, I asked someone to *Tell Me How Long the Train's Been Gone*. I'm still waiting but it hasn't yet returned.

American history is a lie. Not by deliberate misinformation but by omission. It omits mention of the significant contributions people of color have made to this nation. It attempts to render us invisible but finds that it can't. Yet it tries even in the face of its failure.

If Beale Street Could Talk, Nobody Knows My Name, No Name on the Street, Going to Meet the Man, and *The Devil Finds Work* were all written to give voice to a people who refused to be silenced.

Mine is one in many and I try to raise it loud and clear as I did so many years ago as a boy in my father's church.

I started out in gospel then moved on to the blues. But as you can see, I never really left gospel and I'm singing it now before you hoping that you'll all join in.

A writer has only one voice. But that's a start. A preacher has one voice, too. When the writer becomes the preacher or the preacher becomes the writer you have the hybrid that stands before you now.

I was asked to come here and speak of my life and I think I have. My life thus far has been one long wait. Waiting for the dream of America's deliverance to become a reality. . . . And I'm still waiting.

Thank you for coming and listening to me.

He exits.

Performance Rights